AF447373

Contents

To God the Father,
Who made me as I am

To Dad James and Mom Carolyn,
Who raised me as I am

To My Darling Felacia,
Who accepts me as I am

To Caleb and Eve,
Who show me who I can be

INTRODUCTION

THE ROOT OF ANGER

I can distinctly remember the first time I got angry.

In fact, it's one of my earliest memories. The years were 1978-79. I was five years old. We were staying with some friends of the family for about two weeks after having to prematurely move out of a house my parents just sold. To a five-year-old, adult details mean very little, and I was no exception. I just remember riding in the back seat of the car, hearing Dad and Mom talk about going to a party that some friends from our church were having. Of course, I wanted to go, and I said so. That's what five-year-olds who don't know that there are places they can't go will say. Dad told me I wasn't going to be able to go, but that I'd be staying with Janet and her kids Ricky and Becky. I recall Janet being a very nice, kind lady (She let a Family of four live with her for two weeks!), and Ricky and Becky were kind, good kids to me, so I didn't have issues with staying with her. I just wanted to go with Mom and Dad.

When Dad said no, even at that young age, something triggered in me. Perhaps it was the finality of it. Perhaps it wasn't getting my way.

Perhaps as a young parent of maybe 26 years old, Dad may have said "No" in the harsh way a young parent under the stresses of moving and selling houses and adult stuff would. I don't know what it was that triggered me. But I can vividly remember becoming furious. So furious in fact that I determined that as soon as we got home, I was going to run away because it wasn't fair. As soon as the car stopped in the driveway, that's what I did. I took off as fast as I could run. I had befriended a kid up the street from Janet's house, and I ran headlong to his front door. I beat on the front door until he and his mom came to the door, and I asked his mom if I could live with them. I don't recall their reaction, but I'm sure my friend's mother was shocked. Then Dad came around the corner, calling my name.

I was bound and determined that I was not going to go home with him, so I started climbing on a metal latticework support near the front door. I was going to climb onto the roof and refuse to come down! I was not going home with Dad. It seems funny now, a five-year-old child thinking he could just climb on the roof of a house and live there just to get away from his anger. But I knew that's what I was going to do. Dad caught me of course before I made it very far up the lattice, and he carried me writhing and squirming back to the house. Mom told me she'd never seen me act like that, both legs kicking and arms flailing in fury. She said my response scared her, and Dad as well.

Naturally, as a non-denominational Christian family, the Bible says spare the rod and spoil the child, so I got a good whuppin'... it's as if they thought a demon had taken me over, and it had to be driven out. Dad spanked me with his belt in the bedroom we were staying in. What I remember most is this: we were probably in there for half an hour, but for what seemed like hours to me, I refused to cry. Dad would spank with the belt a few times, then he would ask me if I was going to be obedient. He seemed to be quite afraid of the way I was reacting, because I was determined not to break. I was too angry! He was praying to God for whatever was going on in my head, spanking me, and talking at the same time. I know for a fact that I didn't break until I decided to break. I don't know what inside of me released me to give in. It wasn't pain, or tiredness, or lack of resolve. I think I realized it was hopeless to resist. I was the quintessential marginalized person, a kid with no power. Then I started to cry. Feeling like you have no power makes you feel despondent, depressed, and angry. When I started crying, Dad stopped spanking me. And he started crying. I could tell he was relieved that I finally gave in. I think I was relieved too. It takes a tremendous amount of personal energy to stay angry all the time, and an intense amount of energy to be furious like I was that day. Mom told me that I never acted that way before... and that I never acted that way with them since.

And that's what bothers me now.

Where did all that anger go? Unresolved anger is not a vapor that just evaporates away; it's a cancer that spreads throughout the body and the mind, far and wide, hiding in every crack and corner it can find. It doesn't just go away. I think about my own son. When he was a two- and three-year-old boy, I was just a bit older than my Dad was when I ran away, and I was just as immature in parenting as he was. Now, our son has a certain condition that causes him pain at various times, depending on conditions and how he cares for himself. He was born with it. I recall as a young father that there were times that he was crying as a little boy, that he was probably in a pain crisis.

He didn't know what was going on, but he knew something in his body was hurting him. I didn't know what to ask him, but I knew he wasn't being "Obedient" or "Doing as he was told". I would spank him sometimes because he cried too much, not realizing what his little body might have been going through. I can count on one hand how many times I have spanked our son or our daughter. I wouldn't have considered myself an abusive parent. I can recall very few times that my Dad or Mom spanked me. So I wouldn't have considered Dad or Mom to have been abusive parents. Yet deep down, I greatly regret the frustration and anger that led me to spank my little three-year-old boy for what was probably something as simple as him having a pain crisis from a disease he had no control over. By society's standards, I may not have been considered an abusive parent or an abusive husband, yet somewhere inside, I feel like that deep root of anger that I had, and still struggle with, did damage to my son and my daughter in one form or another, and it has done damage in my marriage to Felacia, as well. Again, I ask, where did all that anger go?

That is the purpose of this book.

I don't have all the answers, but I hope somewhere in my journey to figure out some of the places where anger was born in me, and where it still festers, I can figure out how to let it all go. I have titled this book "An Angry Man" because I don't have a corner on the market of anger. I'm only one angry man, but there are billions of angry men and angry women. The world is full of it... ate up with it like we say in the Deep South. And as uncontrolled anger always has, it's killing us.

CHAPTER 1

SOAKED IN THE PAST, POISONING THE FUTURE

The second place I can remember being connected to my young propensity for anger was church. Next to family, church was our most important and significant institution. Why would I not say Jesus or God? That's not a simple answer, even though it is a simple question. I strongly believe to many in the Christian church, Jesus and the church were and are interchangeable. We were all in church because of Jesus, and we were all in Jesus because of church. Having matured in my faith at the age of 50, I have gained more and more clarity in the fact that the church as we know it exists because of Jesus Christ, yet it is its own unique institution. It has a humanity of its own, a life of its own, and the church is very fallible and very sinful. As the Body of Christ on this earth, the church is made up of we humans, with all the struggles and fallacies that come with being human. To a great degree, Jesus was constantly assaulted by the church of His day, and that was part of what He came to save us from. The institutions that surrounded the church in His time made him angry, so much so that He went into the temple and flipped tables over!

Honestly, any institution created by man has the potential to create disillusionment and anger in the people who are raised up under its umbrella. Unfortunately, the church is no different. One of my earliest memories of anger was not really mine, but it became mine later. My parents had become a part of the church where they first met as young teenagers in a youth group in the mid-1970s. They met young, married young, and had me as their first child very young. I would venture to say the church we were in would have been considered a mega church in New Orleans at the time, if such a concept existed back then, and these were young people who were a part of the Jesus Movement that swept the country in the '70s. The Word of Faith movement was beginning to take hold, and our church was exciting and growing. I was five or six at the time, so most of that made little difference to me. But during those next few years, I can remember little things. I remember leaving the big church, which was relatively multicultural, and we began to go to a new, young church started by one of the other men who came up in the youth group with my parents. At the new church, our pastor was black, as opposed to the big church, where the pastor was white. The new church was in a different part of town. The new church was all black, and a lot of our family on my mom's side attended there.

These events were the natural progression of life. And I was still very young. I watched Sesame Street, and Electric Company, and Mr. Rogers... life for me as a kid was pretty simple. My parents kept a safe, good home for us, drama free as far as we were concerned. My little brother Nathan was born, so now there were two of us. It was pleasant being a kid. As I got older however, little seeds of anger and an unknown cloud began to descend, from things that I didn't understand, but somehow knew I should feel anger about. Dad and Mom both had beautiful singing voices, and Dad studied opera in college, so I remember them doing music ministry in the young church. The new pastor eventually started a church school, and my very young father was the principal for a short period. My parents were very involved, even though my Dad had a very good job at the phone company and Mom was a nurse. At some point, our lives began to transition, and Dad wasn't working at the phone company. And by the late '70s, something happened with the young church, and we weren't attending there anymore. In fact, we left New Orleans and moved to Lafayette, Louisiana for a while.

We spent most of my and my sibling's elementary and teenage years moving to new cities, and often new states. I never knew exactly what happened at the young church until many years later, but somehow, I knew what happened was wrong, that Mom and Dad had been mistreated, and that I should be angry. Living in a world of Mr. Rogers and Oscar the Grouch, I had few reasons to be angry at the time(except when I ran away from home at the age of five 'cause I was mad), so much of my anger was misplaced and vague. I think one of the most dangerous kinds of anger is vague anger. You're angry at someone or something, but whatever you're angry at is a shadowy figure who doesn't come out into the light. These are opaque, unclear enemies... like the government.... White people... Black people.... Rich people.... Poor people... Young people.... Old people... I didn't know why I should be angry, but I knew something had been done unjustly, and Mom and Dad were the victims.

To me, the roots of vague anger often begin in childhood for all of us as humans, from people, places or events that affected us or our families in a negative way, which then tend to seep into our young world and slowly poison our worldview. I don't think it's ever intentional on the part of parents that life itself transfers its woes to us children, just like it was never intentional when my own anger seeped over into my son and my daughter. It's just a part of being a part of someone else. There is a passage in the Bible that I find very sad but very telling. King David is dying and preparing to pass the kingdom on to his son Solomon. David gives Solomon a lot of great advice about kingship and its pitfalls. He encourages his son to seek God for kingly wisdom and for the ability to lead Israel well. But firmly seated in David's admonitions to the new young king were two weighty and unfair tasks to fulfill after his death: "Now you yourself know what Joab son of Zeruiah did to me—what he did to the two commanders of Israel's armies, Abner son of Ner and Amasa son of Jether. He killed them, shedding their blood in peacetime as if in battle, and with that blood he stained the belt around his waist and the sandals on his feet. Deal with him according to your wisdom, but do not let his gray head go down to the grave in peace. And remember, you have with you Shimei son of Gera, the Benjamite from Bahurim, who called down bitter curses on me the day I went to Mahanaim. When he came down to meet me at the Jordan, I swore to him by the Lord: 'I will not put you to death by the sword.' But now, do not consider him innocent. You are a man of wisdom; you will know what to do to him. Bring his gray head down to the grave in blood."-1 Kings 2:5-6,8-9.

David obviously had reasons that he felt betrayed by both Joab and Shimei, and his anger at both men was quite possibly with great cause. What was not with great cause, however, and what was tremendously unfair, was that David tasked his son Solomon to execute his revenge on these men after his death, and these men who were most likely as old and gray and weary in their sins and mistakes as David himself was. David was soon to die. Why pass his bitterness and rage on to his son?

I believe we as parents often do this to our children without realizing it. We are angry about some injustice in life, and we unwittingly roll it over to children who weren't there and have no idea why they should be angry. But because they love us, and are following our lead, they become angry too. A child can become steeped in anger like a bag of tea steeping in a teacup. My wife Felacia loves to steep her Sleepytime Tea in a teacup right before bed, covering the rim of the cup with a coaster and letting the tea infuse into the hot water. It takes a few minutes, but the golden hue of the tea slowly begins to seep and swirl into the water. By the time she climbs into bed, the tea is ready. An angry child is like that steeping tea; over time, slights and injustices faced by either parent can infuse into anger in a child, even if the parent hasn't directly expressed any anger to them.

For example, my Dad was adopted as a baby because my grandmother was made to adopt him off by my grandfather. Granddad felt they had too many kids. So, Grandma arranged for Mr. and Mrs. Woods to adopt him. Although the Woods were good parents, Dad once told me he always wanted to know his own family. Eventually as a young man, he and his mother were able to get in contact with each other. Many years later, in an effort for Dad and for us to get to know his biological family, our family of five moved to California and lived with my grandmother and grandfather in their house. Along with us, my aunt and her three kids and my maternal great-grandfather lived there. All five of us Woods stayed in one of the rooms in grandma's house. Both Mom and Dad managed to get very good jobs in California, but even in the late 1980s, California was an outrageously expensive place to live. Needless to say, all those people in the house was tremendously awkward for everyone; I hated the school I was attending, my brother and sister didn't like their elementary school, and we as kids could feel the overall tension... it was not the dream my father imagined.

In hindsight, I realize how gracious it was for Grandma and Grandpa to let us all live with them like that for six whole months. I can't imagine how stressful that must have been for them to have a houseful of adults and young children and an old great grandfather who stayed drunk and watched baseball all day. I became extra bitter during that time. I was angry that Dad didn't have the dream reunion he expected with the parents he'd always imagined. I was angry that we had to live somewhere we weren't wanted for six months. I was angry that we moved all the time. I was angry that Grandma didn't want us. I learned later that my Grandfather was not a very good man to his family, quite abusive in fact, and I later became thankful that God in His amazing way spared my Dad from the life he could have had. For a long time after we moved away from California, I stayed very angry at my Dad's biological family, especially Grandma. I believe I was most angry at her because deep down I know she really cared for my Dad and she didn't want to give him up. She was made to. So, she tried to reconnect as best as she could with her son and his family. Those reunions are never perfect and almost always messy.

I eventually had to resolve that staying angry at my Grandparents in proxy for my Dad was immature and unfair. I was beginning to become that person who looks for anything that anyone could have possibly done to wrong him, to use that bitterness as a life preserver. I was trying to stay afloat on my anger, but misplaced anger is always a rock that quickly causes you to sink and drown in your unforgiveness. There was a point in that journey that I realized that becoming like the bitter, mean men my grandfather and great grandfather had been was going to eventually be my story as well, and in many ways, it was for a long time. My father didn't pass a torch of bitterness to me as David tried to do to Solomon. Dad was just trying to find himself. I just added my own bitterness to what I perceived as a slight against me personally. A bitter person is usually a selfish person, who sees every slight, whether against himself or someone he cares about, as an offense against him that should be marked for all eternity. And that sort of a person becomes the sort of person who begins to hurt others in the pursuit of no longer getting hurt. I didn't want to become that mean, bitter vindictive man I imagined my Grandfather to be, but something had to change. I couldn't continue to poison my future.

Some years later, I wrote a poem about what I believed that poisoning of my soul was doing to me, and I'd like to share it here:

The Thing in My Chair

A Thing

Is sitting

In my chair,

Occupying my seat

As I feed it

My grievances.

The Thing is Flesh,

Neither human,

Nor animal, nor plant;

Just an ugly mass of tissue

And black wiry hairs

And ruddy skin,

With only one

Identifiable orifice:

An ever-open mouth,

Constantly chewing.

It is a gaping, sustenance-soiled Maw.

The Thing sits

(slouches really,

for it has no backbone

to hold it erect)

as I feed it.

It sits

In my God-given seat

Of authority.

It occupies

My rightful seat

Because I placed

It there;

I feed it

And pet it

And coddle it,

This disgusting,

Lobotomized mass

Of flesh,

Like it was

My pet Shih-Tzu.

I name it Offense,

And I let it occupy

The chair of

God's plan for me,

All the while

Wondering why

God won't use me.

....

I am very glad to say that today there are far less intruders sitting in my chair, or any of the chairs at my table, which leaves a lot of room for friends and family to occupy those spaces. My resolve not to feed the anger of the past has left me with great relief for a good future, and much more peace for the present.

CHAPTER 2

SO INFAMOUS, YOU'VE A SHIRT NAMED AFTER YOU

There is no creature on this earth, no entity in this universe, or the ones unseen, that can create so much passion, be it rage, lust, or the deepest love, as a woman can create in her man. And there is no creature on earth, indeed in all of God's great creation, that wears a ring on its finger, that can embolden or enrage that man dubbed husband, as the woman that he has committed to name his "wife".

If there is an archetypical angry man, I would lay all the odds that the heading above his picture would say The Angry Husband. This mythical creature is so known, so famous, that he even has the style of shirt that I would gather 99% of Americans know under one name: "The Wifebeater". Any time I've ever heard that item of clothing called by this name, I knew exactly what they were talking about. He was wearing a white tank top, most likely an undershirt, and inevitably, I could describe the man himself: a huge pot belly, food stains on his shirt, heavy five o'clock shadow, unkempt... slovenly... loud... disgusting. This man I believe would be the dictionary definition of an angry husband, a man so angry at the world, at his position in life, at his job, at his station in the order of things that he takes all his rage out on his meek little wife and poor, terrified kids.

In all my 24 years of marriage to my sweet wife, I always prided myself on not being this man. I swore to myself that I wouldn't beat her or even hit her. I wouldn't shove her. We wouldn't have screaming arguments in front of our children. I wouldn't rage around the house at the slightest provocation. I was not going to be that man. And for the most part, I was not that man, not in the way that I imagined him to be. Yet, as I look back, in my own deeper way, I was very much that angry man, that seething, enraged husband around whom the whole family seemed to tread lightly on those ever so delicate eggshells. And I didn't even realize it.

I believe, and I think Felacia would say, that I put on a pretty good show of being the calm, even-tempered, nice guy I always imagined myself to be. I'm a 9 on the enneagram, which is labeled as the Peacemaker, and I would venture to say that I truly was a peacemaker. The only problem with being a peacemaker is that one is generally only making peace for oneself. That kind of peace is not the kind made for everyone in the vicinity. I made peace for me. That kind of peace is often very exclusionary to the people I find myself around, especially my own family. It's never intended to be that way. The exclusion of others comes as a result of selfishness and a deep need for self-preservation.

There are a lot of background details about our early days of marriage that I won't go into here, and many of them are detailed in my previous book "The Princess and The Dragon", which I wrote when I thought I was a marriage expert and published in 2019. As someone so skillful at marriage as to have written a book on it, I would never have imagined that three years later, we as a married couple would have been right at the very precipice of divorce, so close that I could feel the icy winds of defeat swirling at the edge beneath my toes. But back to the beginning.

It was our wedding night, just after our reception at the meeting hall in the little Alabama town where Felacia is from. Most of the festivities were over, and the night was wrapping up. My bride and I were going to have a one-night stay at a bed and breakfast in New Orleans, and then we'd be returning to Alabama for work the following Monday. I, of course, paid for absolutely nothing for our wedding. She paid for my tux, my brother's and my cousin's tux, her dress, my ring, and our apartment that I was already living in... basically, I just showed up. So, you can only imagine the swirl of feelings she must have been having as a young bride, on what has always been hailed as one of the greatest days of a woman's life, but instead finding herself footing all the bills for a 26-year-old new husband, who was still four years her senior. I imagine deep down her red flag radar was screaming "RUN, RUN!!!!!" at the top of its hoarse voice.

We were preparing to follow my parents to the bed and breakfast. The owner was a friend of my Dad's, and he and Mom paid for the night's stay. And, unbeknownst to us, Mom and Dad also paid to rent a nice Cadillac sedan to drive themselves down to our wedding. It was a beautiful white car, and I was very impressed. The problem was this: Dad, in his eager but often over-assumptive fashion, rented the car with the goal that he and Mom would chauffeur us in the Caddy to the bed and breakfast, while my brother and sister trailed us in our car. Neither my sweet, overwhelmed bride or I knew that this was what Dad was planning, but when he told me what he wanted to do, I automatically prepared myself to tell Felacia what the plan was. I was oblivious to the idea that she would have any objections whatsoever... How immensely stupid and immature I was! We had just married! I'm sure she imagined a giddy ride together in her new Nissan Altima, now our new Nissan Altima. We would ride together and talk and laugh about the events of the day, the good, the bad, and the weird; it would be our first night together as man and wife. We both were anticipating what was to come later: our first complete sexual experience other than a kiss here and there, and the true end of our virginity.

I know that I totally ignored how she felt, not intentionally, but uncaringly. I got angry that she even suggested that she'd rather not ride with them. I'm sure I told her she was being unfair and inconsiderate of the money they spent to rent the car. I don't remember everything I said to dissuade her from wanting to drive our own car together, but I do know that I got mad enough, pouted hard enough, that she gave in. She gave in that night, but she was hurt, very deeply, almost irrevocably hurt that I chose to value my Dad's feelings over hers. It was a sign to her young emotions of what was to come between us. It wasn't until the very tangible possibility of divorce in early 2022 and some therapy I got during that time, that I began to realize what I had done to her all those years ago. The subject would come up at what I deemed random times over the years, and I would often suggest that she blindsided me all the time with my mistakes of the past; I never quite understood what it was about that incident that hurt her so deeply. It wasn't until I asked myself why I did what I did that night that everything began to make sense.

I was a very late bloomer in starting my adult life. I graduated with an English degree (perhaps the most useless of all degrees ever known to man unless you're going to be a teacher or a lawyer) after five years of lollygagging, and I was probably 25 years old when I finally moved out of Mom and Dad's house. When I met Felacia, I had only been in my small cave of an apartment about six months. She thought I'd been out on my own for quite a while, experiencing the world for much longer than I actually had been. I was freshly bathing in the realm of freedom, the world of adult autonomy, where my decisions were my own, as were my mistakes. As a grown man who was still very used to being an outwardly obedient child, I still felt the pressure to obey my parents. As a man, there should be no notion of obedience to your parents if you don't live with them. The whole idea should be strange and foreign. But not doing what Dad told me to do instead felt strange and foreign to me.

It was this vague and unknown pressure, the pressure to do what I was told, that made me so angry that night, very coerced in ways that I felt very deeply but couldn't explain then, that led me to channel that anger over to my young wife, whom I now labeled as being very inconsiderate. If only I had realized that it was actually my father who was being inconsiderate without meaning to be, who was doing something he thought was a nice gesture, though in reality, it was ill-timed. I believe had I realized that at the time, and gently confronted him, he would have understood, and he would have respected it. And Felacia would have felt safe and protected by me, something I don't think that she felt for most of our marriage. I often imagine that whole event as the great climactic scene in a movie, where the hero rushes in to rescue the lady... but instead he trips over a rock and smashes his head on the ground, laying there unconscious. And the credits roll.

That night was truly a watershed moment for me, and especially for us as a couple. It was actually a few years into our marriage when I slowly began to see myself as the man of my house and not a boy in my

Dad's house. We were attending a church in town, and Mom and Dad came down from New Orleans to visit the church there in Mobile. They really liked it, and they liked the pastor. Felacia and I decided that we were going to attend a different church, for reasons that were our own, and by a decision made in tandem by the two of us. I recall talking to my Dad about the decision to go to the other church. He told me he disagreed with our choice and to my immature mind, he was upset, and I was "in trouble". As we talked, I began to tick off various things to myself in my mind: we were paying a mortgage. We both worked good jobs. We paid all our utilities with our own money. We owned one car outright and were paying for the other. We were adults. I was a man. And I was the man of my own house (although not a great one at that point). The decision about what church to attend was ours to make. Dad didn't like the decision, but in the end, he accepted it. At that point, I very, very slowly began to turn a corner in my manhood. I believe what creates angry husbands is also what often creates angry men: the indirect, unseen assault on the notion of what being a man is. Oftentimes, I think men deep down believe their wives, and women in general, always see the deepest parts of who they feel they are, and that deep down they are scared little boys who don't have all the answers. I sometimes wonder if that's why some of these modern men decide they want to be women, and some others buy elaborate collie suits to live out a secret fantasy of being a dog. Some men will do anything in the effort to not have to face manhood.

I know for my part, I spent a healthy portion of our marriage wrestling for significance with Felacia, trying to prove to her that I was a capable man, who could make life happen for both of us. I think she just wanted to be with the Joel she dated, who cared about how she felt and what she thought about the world and her place in it, the guy who just enjoyed being with her, riding in that old '93 Chevy Cavalier, just to see where we would end up.

Finding that man, the adventurer to whom the world was wide open, has become my resolve for these next 25 years together. We have lost so many years being angry at each other and at situations beyond our control that in many ways, it has left us both exhausted. Developing friendships and connections can be challenging, and it can seem like a herculean effort to reach out, to extend ourselves beyond our borders. The first step in that journey for us was to tear down walls and barriers to each other. That has allowed us to grab hands and begin to walk together, meeting good people along the way. Needless to say, the second step was to change out of that grimy, filthy tank top of offense and anger, taking a bath in grace and forgiveness, and putting on the robes of righteousness. These new clothes are so much softer and cleaner, and they smell so much better!

CHAPTER 3

ANGER IS A JUNK DRAWER

Recently, I listened to a message by Chip Ingram called "Overcoming Emotions that Destroy-Part 2: Why We All Struggle with Anger", and within less than a minute of his teaching, he enlightened me about something I never knew about anger. It was so life-changing in fact that I am going to regurgitate it back to you right now.

He said anger is a secondary emotion.

Just that simple phrase, that one idea, helped me see my struggles with anger totally opposite of what I had been seeing them before. I'll give some history first. I truly believe since the incident when I was five and tried to run away from home, I began to think that my best recourse with any strong emotion was to stuff it. Chip Ingram said people are either Stuffers, Leakers, or Exploders. I'm definitely a Stuffer. I believe we are all three at any given time, but one dominates. Stuffing my emotions became my dominant way to deal with them. I would often feel a certain way about something that was said or done, but I rarely spoke up. I would sulk, get quiet, retreat to the cave. I avoided confronting the person, or the issue. It was just easier.

I got to be really good at stuffing my emotions. I had a co-worker a few years ago, who, every time I saw him, would say, "Joel is the nicest guy in the refinery". There was a time that such compliments made me proud, because that meant no one was seeing my real feelings, which I equated with being Godly. But by that point, I would often say, "I wish I was as nice as people think I am." That was so true for me. I wished I was a nicer person. I had stuffed for so long that I really spent a lot of my energy avoiding people. Felacia has been my opposite when it comes to people. She is the type of person who enters a room and it's like a sunbeam has entered with her. She lights up any space she enters. And when we were young married, she really enjoyed people and having people over. Especially family. I gave her such a terrible time about it, because I was always too tired and didn't feel like company, that it eventually got to the point where she no longer enjoyed company herself. My anger had become a junk drawer and being around different people was like rummaging through that drawer looking for some things, some emotions, that I didn't want to be found.

I worked hard to come across as a nice person, but the effort to do so, to be non-threatening, was taking a heavy toll on me. It was taking a heavy toll on our marriage. I was trying to be the definition of a nice person, agreeable and pleasant, but most times I failed miserably in front of the people to whom it mattered most: my family. I had become a person who held grudges, deep grudges like a trench in the soul, a person who would quickly write people off my nice list if they bothered me or crossed certain lines that I felt were sacred. I didn't like people who talked incessantly because I thought they were self-centered and always wanted to be heard. That was because I was really feeling the emotion of not being heard, that my voice wasn't important. I didn't like people that I felt bragged a lot. I felt they were overconfident and lacked humility. But really, I felt my own lack of confidence, so confident people annoyed me. Felacia always seemed very confident to me, but actually she's just very genuine. She's the most genuine person I know. There were times when she would say something that hurt my feelings, and because I developed a habit of competing with her, I would assume she intentionally said whatever she said to hurt me. In her genuine and honest nature, I've had to learn that a lot of the things I thought she said to be hurtful really hurt because of my own open emotional sores, not because she was trying to hurt me. I was the kid who took his ball and went home when he got angry. I've found peace with the realization that I'm not a nice person. I can be mean, sometimes petty, and oftentimes selfish even on my best days; there are so many negatives I can mention!

I can imagine you're thinking, "How depressing! Where is the hope in that?" I found that admitting these things to myself, along with coming to the realization that I struggle with anger, was a massive relief for me. I'm coming from a space of very rigid Christian morality, where it seemed like it was not so important to truly be like Christ as long as you looked Christlike to other people. The notion that getting angry about things wasn't always a bad thing, that anger could be a toilet instead of a junk drawer, was foreign to me. Healthy anger could be a place where unhealthy emotions are dealt with, and then flushed, not piled high and closed off, never to be dealt with. It was liberating to realize that Jesus Himself got angry, and he expressed his anger in Matthew 21:12-13, entering the temple of God in Jerusalem:

"Jesus entered the temple area and drove out all who were buying and selling there. He overturned the tables of the money changers and the benches of those selling doves. 'It is written,' he said to them, 'My house will be called a house of prayer, but you are making it a den of robbers. '" Jesus was angry, but His real emotion was love and passion, love for the people who came to worship in the temple in true and real faith. He got angry because he was confronted by opportunists and thieves, who were there to make a buck. He made His anger active, to create change. Anger is a kinetic emotion. It should always be related to action. Anger when channeled properly can create real change.

Life has shown me that sometimes you overturn tables, and sometimes you make a table. The same Jesus that overturned tables is the same Jesus that later created a table for His disciples in Matthew 26. I believe He realized that changing the hearts of those who wittingly or unwittingly hurt others can only happen by changing the hearts of people who want to change. I spent a lot of my time being angry at people over the years who I thought slighted me, but I was turning into a person who was unintentionally slighting others. There's a true healing in becoming that person who sets a table and invites others to join them. Emotions are the feasts of the mind, and I think setting a table to sort through those emotions, good or bad, is healing for the soul. Christ's need to set a table with His disciples one last time was a need for Him to process some things emotionally with them before He went to the cross. Men, we don't do that enough! The brave man processes the feelings that will hinder his bravery before he goes to battle, so that his sword will strike true. Instead of using healthy ways to deal with our feelings, we can become like an emotional colostomy bag with a small puncture in it. All of our little annoyances and frustrations begin to seep out of the bag any time that the bag is put under pressure, and the waste products of our emotions become messy to us, and the people around us. Emotional constipation becomes uncontained. Eventually, if we're not careful, those emotions create so much pressure that the bag explodes on ourselves and anyone in the vicinity. I have had those emotional colostomy ruptures of anger before, and I remember each of them well.

My kids haven't seen me constantly get angry, at least not openly. But the times they remember, they remember very well. I am sure they remember the quiet awkwardness of a person who isn't comfortable with his feelings of anger or frustration, but my son still reminds me of a time I got really angry at Felacia. I sold a particular item to my brother-in-law for $200 and he was going to give me the funds at a later point. The funds were conveyed via my sister-in-law to Felacia, who put them in the bank. Meanwhile, I had been looking for the money to deposit but never saw it. Felacia is the studious one when it comes to our bank accounts, so I asked her if an extra $200 had come into our bank account one evening when I got in from work. Our son was in the room nearby watching tv. Felacia told me the money had come in via her sister, and it was already used on groceries or something to that effect. To give some context, I was in a period in my life that I believe was a bit of a mid-life crisis, where I had begun to feel a bit used, like all I was good for was making money and that everyone in the house was taking my hard work for granted. So, I must honestly say that I had a chip on my shoulder about this money. In fact, I had been cultivating the chip for a while. I was already preparing myself to get angry if I discovered the money had been spent in any way. When Felacia told me the money had come in and she had spent it, I went from 0 to Angry in 2 seconds, yelling at her as to how she thought she could spend money that wasn't hers to spend and not everything that comes into the house goes to pay bills. I was furious, and I made sure she knew it. My son and daughter knew it too before all was said and done and because I had not practiced healthy expressions of my emotions, my junk drawer was full. The colostomy bag was packed tight. The emotional baggage was overweight, and everyone in the house was paying the cost.

I now know that at the time, I was feeling the pressures of being the sole breadwinner of the home, with a son about to graduate, insurance on several vehicles, preparing to send kids to college, mortgages, job stresses.... Life piles up in the junk drawer, and if we don't find healthy ways to offset the pressure, we will explode in the wrong ways. So I exploded on Felacia, and the residue spackled her and my kids like paint overspray. We often laugh about it now because my fit of anger was so awkward that my kids can imitate what I said and the way I said it like it's a comedy routine. My true feelings were those of being overwhelmed and underappreciated; my resolve should have been to talk about how I felt instead of just getting angry over one incident. Felacia wasn't trying to spend my money. She had always had to juggle our bills, thus anything that came in, she was immediately trying to figure out where to put it. I had gotten pretty creative at figuring out ways to get the money we needed, but not trying to think much beyond that point. I always left that to her to figure out.

Eventually, I came up with a plan to reduce some of our expenses by moving the family out of our house and into an apartment for a time. My son was headed to college, so it would only be the three of us at home, Felacia and I and our daughter. The plan was a good one, but one huge mistake I made was related to these unresolved emotions of feeling underappreciated. We made a good sum of money on the sale of our home, and I had resolved that I was going to reward myself using some of the proceeds to buy my old 1992 Dodge W250, an old Cummins diesel pickup truck I had been wanting. I told Felacia what I was going to do. She wasn't against the idea, and I had covertly been watching the online ads for a good Dodge for several months. Finally I settled on one in Ohio and put a $500 down payment on it. I flew to Ohio, caught an Uber to the small dealership, and drove the truck home to Alabama. I was trying to satiate the notion that I wasn't able to spend my money like I wanted to by buying something big that I wanted. I want the truck, I work hard, so I'm going to buy the truck. Yet it was OUR money, not just mine! That unresolved emotion of overwhelm has gotten expensive. The truck is a good one, but it came with a lot of its own baggage: bad rust issues from the salted roads of Ohio, loads of electrical issues, non-working air conditioning. There were a myriad of problems that I couldn't see and didn't investigate. I didn't really care, even to the point of ignoring her admonition to buy a similar truck that was in Washington state that was probably in much better condition. And $2000 cheaper. I was just determined to prove I could do what I wanted to do as a man.

I still have the old truck to this day, but it is a constant reminder of the perils of an overfilled emotional junk drawer. Those unresolved emotions can lead you to do some foolish things. Sometimes, it's buying an old truck and sinking almost as much money as you paid for it into fixing it. Sometimes it might be an affair. Sometimes it can be estrangement from family or losing a good friendship. A lot of hurt and tragedy rests in our lack of action in regard to our feelings. It's not wrong to feel; it is dangerous to ignore what you feel. I have decided I want to live my life processing my feelings, so I can live beyond them. I want to get past the secondary to the primary. Every good junk drawer needs to be cleaned out occasionally. Sometimes, your healing is buried in its contents.

CHAPTER 4

MY BLACK CARD HAS EXPIRED

When exactly did my black card expire?

No, I'm not talking about the elusive and legendary black credit card that people who have stellar credit get offered. This black card is even more elusive, and even more legendary. No one has ever seen it, I've not ever had one pulled out of a wallet in front of me, nor do I remember ever feeling like I had been issued one, except for a brief period when I was attending Metro State College of Denver way back in 1991-1993 or thereabouts. I feel like I had a temporary Black card when I minored in African American studies at MSCD for a period before I swapped to a university to finish out my studies. Honestly, I'm not sure why it's a Black card instead of an African-American card, but I do recall an opinion I once heard that Black people in America are not truly African-Americans in the truest sense of the word. Elon Musk as a native South African has more claim to that title than I do.

And there's the rub. Black is a color. No more, no less. Technically, a Black person is not Black of skin per se. We are darker-skinned than many of our brothers and sisters, but "White" people aren't really white. They are lighter-skinned than some other members of the human race. Both terms are truly just constructs to describe people. More so than that, both terms are really constructs to imprison and enslave people. Those terms don't just enslave Black people. They enslave all people because they create boundaries in which it can be very hard to move or be yourself.

Many Black people born in America don't have a sense of connection to Africa as a home, though many of us as we study history begin to develop a sense of place and pride as we read and hear stories about the place our ancestors hailed from. Black Americans, unfortunately, have had to create our own sense of history and place for ourselves in a country where being "Black" was a handicap. I believe creating this sense of Black history and Black placement led to the need for the mythical "Black Card" by which we as Black people in America get "Credit" for being "Black Enough". In a sense, the Black Card is a "Credit" card.

The problem I always met as a child and as a young man, and one I've had to learn to resolve as a man nearing middle age is this: I was not, and still wouldn't be considered "Black" enough. My skin color has never drastically changed from the day I was born until today, so what does that mean? What does it mean to be "Black" enough? And what does any of this have to do with being an angry man? We'll get to that shortly. Let's address the issue of being Black enough. I recently had a conversation with some guys at work about movies. We were talking about the movie "American Gangster". The film stars Denzel Washington in the true story of a man named Frank Lucas, telling Lucas' story of smuggling heroin into the US on American service planes during the Vietnam War, according to Wikipedia. I personally have not seen the movie although I'm a Denzel fan. To give some context about my work environment, we are a crew of eight guys, two of whom are Black, and the rest white. We all get along pretty well, and for the most part have had few issues come up overtly about race. Anyhow, in talking, everyone was saying how great the movie was, and I happened to mention that I had never seen it. Of course, everyone was amazed that, as a Black person, I've not seen "American Gangster". We'd all had a conversation a few weeks earlier about how I and my other Black co-worker hadn't seen "Training Day", Denzel's arguably most famous role, and the one for which he won an Academy Award. Both my Black co-worker and I would most likely be categorized as "White" Black guys because of our interests, and in fact, one of my White fellow crew members recently told me I was "The Whitest Black guy he ever met", presumably because of how I talk or act? I'm not sure what exactly gave me that title. Of course, none of these comments were ever meant in malice, and as I have matured over the years, I've learned not to take them that way. But I always wondered what criteria I would have had to meet to be considered Black enough.

Here are some of my "Not Black Enough" credentials.

I have only seen "Friday" once. I haven't seen "Training Day" because I really don't want to see Denzel Washington play a bad guy. I haven't seen "Monster's Ball" because I think Halle Berry is a beautiful lady and a great actress, and I hate that her only Academy Award was for a movie where she, one of our modern great Black actresses, had to take her clothes off. I'm sure she's had other movies where her performance was more deserving of an Oscar, and I don't want to see her the way I've heard she was in "Monster's Ball". I like Star Wars and science fiction books. I always liked comic books, and I'm still a fan of Marvel characters and movies. I like Sam Cooke, and love Stevie Wonder's music, but I also like Claude Debussy, and Gustav Holst's "The Planets". I enjoy going to coffee shops with Felacia, even though we're often the only Black people in there. Yet I love hip-hop music and have for a long time. I think liking hip-hop ups my "Credit Limit". But I don't really watch sports, and I've never been into sports, except playing football in the neighborhood as a kid. So maybe that drops my "Credit Score". But a lot of people, Black and White, really don't care what I do or don't like. They're being themselves. The older I get, the more I appreciate those kinds of people. For a long time, I struggled with how I believed people were perceiving me as far as me being Black enough, and that's a prison that's hard to escape from.

Feeling judged for not being Black enough around Black people, and too Black around White people, kept me bound by a lot of deep-seated anger for a long time. The boundaries of what it meant to be Black or to be White seemed to be ever-changing, ever-shifting, and always unclear to me. Where was the room to just BE, to be you, yourself, in whatever form that took? I don't necessarily know when I realized that I felt like I was in a racial no-man's land, but I distinctly remember when I understood that the way I was feeling wasn't good. In 1981, our family moved to Rockford, Illinois so Mom and Dad could become music ministers for a newly ordained Ramah graduate whom I'll call Brother John, and his wife whom I'll call Sister Joan. Brother John and Sister Joan were awesome people, great pastors, and my memories of Rockford are among the finest in my childhood. Unfortunately, a dynamic that would serve to mark most of me and my siblings' young lives was the fact that almost inevitably, we as kids and my parents as adults were often the only black people, or among a very few, in our circles. My Mom and Dad became Christians during the beginnings of what would come to be known as the Word of Faith, or Charismatic, movement in Christianity. So, to us as kids, the way Charismatics did things was the way God did things. And invariably, God didn't do things at all the way Black folks did things.

God didn't necessarily sing the way the Clark Sisters sang, even though my Dad and Mom loved the Clark Sisters. We had to get used to the Imperials, Keith Green, Second Chapter of Acts, and Sandi Patti instead, all artists I love to this day. We didn't really listen to "Black" preachers. The Ramah way (Ramah was the Harvard of Charismatic Christianity, the Bible school everyone wanted to say they graduated from) was not to preach, but to teach the Word. So we listened to Kenneth Copeland, Kenneth Hagin, Oral Roberts... and anyone who was on PTL with Jim and Tammy Bakker. In later years, it was TBN with Paul and Jan Crouch. Those were our icons of the faith. We three kids were products of our environment, just like Mom and Dad had become products of the same environment. Now in no way am I saying our lives were bad or lacking during this time. We were a pretty happy, normal 1980s family. It's just that there was always this shadow, this vague notion of something not being quite good enough, of us as people not being quite good enough.

There were occasional flashes of youthful anger on my part, but I don't recall why. I do recall being asked by some of the kids in our church school if Black people had to comb their hair and wanting to pat mine to see how it felt. I remember a kid asking if my skin color would rub off. I recall one of the moms, when she asked my mom what my science project was about, and mom told her I did it on melanin, asking Mom why I chose that particular subject, like it was a weird choice for a science project. I was excited about my science project because melanin was what made my skin brown, so it partially explained what I was. It wasn't a weird choice for me. The idea that it was seen as a weird choice made me feel strange and out of place. I remember that one of the only other Black families in our church school had a teenage son, who was playing a character in a school play my Dad was directing. My Dad mortified one of the White teen girls who was playing a part in the play, because Dad had the audacity as the director to pair this black guy and this white girl up as boyfriend and girlfriend in the production.

I recall being deeply and quietly heartbroken, without understanding why, when one of my best school friends, whom I'll call Charla, learned that her parents were divorcing. Divorce wasn't too strange, even in Christian circles, but the reason they divorced, was. Charla had sandy blondish hair, but it was very kinky and looked unusual to me for a white girl. It didn't really matter to me: I thought it made my young, soft-spoken friend even more unique. One day, my Dad clarified everything about Charla and the way she looked. Charla's mom was divorcing her Dad because they had recently found out that one of her Dad's parents was half-Black, and Charla's mom couldn't live with the fact that he wasn't who she thought he was, as if he had deceived her on purpose.

I remember feeling sad for Charla. Because now she was going to be different too. Something other. Something else. As I recall, their family left the church and the school altogether and I never saw her again.

The defining moment when I understood that we were an unhealthy kind of different was one summer when my Dad took the three of us to swim at a public pool across town. We lived in what might have been considered the "better" part of town, which I have now realized often means where there were few of us Black folk in the neighborhood, but this pool was in "our" part of town, where most of the Black folks in Rockford were known to live. Dad took the three of us into the locker room to change into our swim gear, but all three of us cried and cried and refused to get into the pool. We were finally in a space where every single kid there was Black like us, and we were crying hysterically. Dad was so disturbed that he loaded us back into the car and drove us back home. He was driving, and he began to sob. He said something to the effect of "What have I done to my kids! Y'all are scared of your own people!"

We had not only gotten the notion, very sneakily and covertly, that we were different, but also that in some unexplainable ways, we weren't good enough. We were too good to swim with the other Black kids that scared us at the pool, but not good enough to totally be ourselves when we were with White kids. Feeling out of place creates fear. And fear creates great anger.

Even at the age of fifty, I still struggle with not being afraid. I'm a relatively big, Black guy, so ostensibly, there isn't much that should scare me. But I do vividly remember those years in Rockford, and always being afraid of the dark. And of being dark. Something changed as I got older, and anger became a very viable alternative to fear, as if Anger was Fear's bigger, stronger, older brother, who was far too mad to be afraid.

What has been my ultimate resolve with all this?

I have resolved to let my Black Card expire. One reason I have let my Black card expire is because I think the American notion of Black and White in regard to people is extremely exclusionary. There are so many people, so many races of people that fall into the abyss between Black and White, and it's childish to relegate people to brown, red, yellow. What worked in the days of "Jesus Loves the little children... red and yellow, black and white" doesn't work now. I don't think it ever has. There was a time a few years ago when I had the privilege to work in Hawaii on Oahu for my job. I was there for six weeks, and the strangest but most peaceful thing about Hawaii other than its tremendous beauty was the feeling that no one could have cared less that I was Black. I didn't see many Black people there (there was an amazing populace of Japanese) but being Black was almost a non-issue. I'd never experienced that before. I imagine there are many parts of the world where being Black, or White, or Russian, or German means very little. Many countries judge their people by ethnicity, even though everyone is similar in skin tone. That is the true beauty of travel; you see the world the way God sees it, in all its variety. It's hard to dislike people when you've seen so many different kinds.

Another reason my Card has expired is because I have resolved to know God in a different way than what I learned Him as a child. Jesus loves people, and the song was right about that. But He also wants people to love each other. That love includes the ability to truly forgive and see people beyond their faults and fallacies. It's so much easier to give the people in your life grace when you see them as God sees them, and you see yourself as you really are. I had a White friend of mine at work tell me he believed that the Bible spoke against interracial marriage because it says people should not be unequally yoked. Now the verse he misquoted is 2 Corinthians 6:14-18 (KJV) which reads, "Be ye not unequally yoked together with unbelievers: for what fellowship hath righteousness with unrighteousness? and what communion hath light with darkness?" This doesn't mention marriage or race, just to be clear. Now, I thought highly of my friend, and he is a genuinely great guy, but for several weeks, I was quietly angry at him about what he believed. I never confronted him about it, and eventually left it to prayer. It turned out that a few months later, his daughter ended up dating a black guy, and they got pregnant. I must say my friend took it very well. Though his daughter and the young man didn't end up staying together, he got a beautiful biracial granddaughter out of the deal, and he loves her just as much as his other grandchildren. Because ultimately, he's a good man. That to me is the Hand of God in people, to see them change before your very eyes.

One final reason I've let my Card expire is because I've decided to be okay with being me. I often say that my favorite person to hang out with is myself. That is because whether you like yourself or not, you are always going to be with you, and not liking who God made you to be is miserable and will create a very angry person. I'm happy to be Black because Black is not defined by the movies I watch or activities I like to do. I like being a man because I can enjoy the arts and art museums and Rachmaninoff, and I can enjoy a scent in Bath and Body Works with Felacia without feeling unmannish, but I can also enjoy the sound of my old Dodge Cummins cranking up or shooting pistols at the range. I'm happy knowing Christ and being a Christian because that doesn't have to mean I'm a hypocrite, or that I must be perfect, or that I can only listen to Hillsong Music. God made us all different for a reason.

I've resolved to let my Black Card expire because I don't just want a Card, I want to own this full Bank called the Life we are given to live. Time is our only currency to spend across the expanse from birth to death, so why would I give myself a "Credit Limit" of Blackness when I'm already a Black man? I think we should all cut our Cards up, shred them and throw them to the wind, and spend our currency called Time being who God made us to be. Let the Black Card expire, and the anger with it.

CHAPTER 5

A PLATFORM OF PAIN

There is a trend I have noticed over the years, a trend that has increased in width, in depth, and in depravity. It is a very subtle, nuanced problem, almost clandestine, like a ninja of emotional scarring. I noticed it in myself over the years as I began to understand and analyze why I was always so angry, and where that anger came from. Where did it start? I know for me, anger started at different times in my young life, from different incidents, in different places, but all those places and spaces of pain and anger seemed to add up, to pile up, into a big steaming mess of mental scat. Mental health is a huge topic these days, especially post-2020, and I believe it should be. Our minds are the repository of our lives, the bank if you will, and what we store there has a huge bearing on the way we see the world and our ability to cope with it. Not so long ago, I had to seek professional therapy for a time, to help me get over the hump of pain and anger I had allowed to build over my then 49 years of life. Therapy is not a bad thing, but there is a caveat to that: let therapy be a crutch, not a wheelchair. Pain can shape us, but we don't need it to define us. What do I mean by pain defining us?

Let me give several examples from my own life. When I was a little boy, the incident we talked about previously with the pastor in New Orleans became a defining pain for me. And for a while, that pain became a platform for me, something I stood on, something that made me who I am. Later, as we began to move to places and environments around the country where we were racially in the minority, my platform became being that lone Black kid who was out of place around a bunch of White kids and White people. That became a defining pain. When I was a teenager, my Dad told us something that happened to him when he was five; it was a trauma that affected not only him, but us as a family for many, many years to come. He joined a group at the time that was for adults who had dealt with that particular kind of trauma, and this was a very defining and healing time for him. I remember he and my Mom sat us three teenage kids down, and Dad opened up about what happened to him, and how it shaped him emotionally as a little kid. I was heartbroken for him, and yet relieved that he was getting it out in the open, beginning to deal with what happened and how he felt. Knowing what happened explained a lot of things for me about my Dad, and why he would get angry at different times during our childhood. While this time period became a healing time for him, I believe I had begun to get quite skillful at creating defining points of pain, and I added it to the pile of things that defined my pain in this life. That pain began to shape who I was. Being an angry young man was becoming a platform.

Dare I add as a small aside this one point: the United States of America has developed a characteristic definition of Black people that

I am determined not to feed into in myself any longer. The definition is this: All Black people in America are angry and should stay angry. That is our defining pain as a people, that we should stay angry for the very real injustices, past and present, that have happened to us in our home, The United States of America. Our news cycle feeds this, our movies, our music, our conversations... all these things peel open a gaping wound that never heals. Scars are good; wounds are not.

Now back to the defining pain. Defining pain, if left unchecked, becomes a platform of pain. What does that mean exactly? Whatever the pain you experienced becomes your platform, the rock you stand on, the hill you die on. How does pain become a platform? I'm a big Marvel and DC fan, so let's find some examples there. Batman is a crimefighter whose platform was what? -the shooting death of his mother and father. One of the hallmarks of the character of Bruce Wayne is that he fights crime continuously in Gotham City, but he never finds healing. Another example: The Punisher, my favorite comic book as a kid. Frank Castle lost his wife and two children in a mob killing in New York, and his whole story centers around finding the men and the structures that killed his family. Revenge is the Punisher's platform. He's an antihero. John Wick is another non-comic book example. He lost his wife, his dog, his car and his home. Basically, he lost a peaceful life and a family after a lifetime of violence, and his revenge on the High Table becomes his platform, and the platform for all those whom the High Table has held hostage. He's an antihero who has become a hero.

I started to notice that some of my favorite heroes in the world of entertainment began to morph from the Spiderman type, who has a tragedy but allows it to shape him into a force for good, or Superman, who is an alien in a strange place as I often felt I was, a hero who decided to use the things that made him different to make a positive change in the world around him. I was becoming fascinated with the antihero, who didn't mind going outside of the law to accomplish justice. When I say law, I'm not talking about the American justice system or any other justice system. I'm talking about the innate moral law that God puts in all humankind. The antihero goes around that kind of law. And I was becoming okay with that, if I am honest. After hearing about the things that happened to my Dad, I began to despise adults that would harm children, sexually, physically, or emotionally. If there was any type of sin or sinner that I thought should be wiped from the face of the earth, it was a child molester. I still think molesting a child is a heinous thing to do, and I always will. There are elements of our society that are trying to normalize the sexualization of children, and we sane adults should fight this tooth and nail for the sake of the children that are here and those yet to come. But I cannot make this into a platform.

The problem with a platform is this: platforms are very narrow, with very defined borders. It is very easy to tumble off your platform to one side or the other, and the people that are surrounding you will eat you alive. Especially any platform that is built on anger. Staying angry takes a tremendous amount of energy, energy that our minds and bodies crave to create real and true changes in our lives and our situations. Platforms are great for memorials, places to remember key times and events. Statues always stand on platforms. We do need to re-member pivotal events, good and bad. How does the saying go? Those who forget the past are doomed to repeat it? Truer words have never been spoken. We don't need to forget. We just don't need to stay there. Felacia said something so brilliant the other day as we were talking that

I must repeat it here; she said it's not good to just be a dreamer because that means you are always asleep. That is so true! Somehow, in our collective and individual pain, we all stay asleep, and continue to be abused by the very forces that feed on us remaining asleep. I've always been whimsical, a dreamer, and quite fanciful, which is okay, but life has still got to be lived. Pain must be addressed if we don't want to stay angry the rest of our lives.

Another problem with a platform of pain is that it tends to morph you into a person who unwittingly begins to cause pain in the people around you. I think this is almost inevitable. Hurting people hurt people, as they say. I know for me, my platform of anger over what happened to my Dad clouded me from seeing a creeping, sneaky, evil demon that plagues our society and our families as much as child abuse: the abuse of women. Mind you, being abusive is not just a male problem; women can be abusive as well. But the abuse of women that has normalized itself in our society for years and years upon end is more subtle than just physical or sexual abuse. It's the abuse in how you view people outside of yourself. I've never been a person who abuses women physically. I've always thought that was equally as heinous as abusing children. But I believe resting on my platform of pain didn't allow me to see ways in which I was still being abusive to my wife. My pouting when I didn't get my way. Stifling her natural bent towards people and connection. It got to a point where I think Felacia felt so stunted and controlled by my moods and secret practices that she was quite ready to just be by herself.

The biggest way, however, that I believe I abused her other than my moods and attitude without really realizing it was through pornography. I am quite sure that many people will disagree that watching porn abuses anyone outside of themselves, but I beg to differ. Just as my Dad was exposed to sexual things far before the time, at a time of great innocence, I too was exposed to sexual things I didn't need to see at a very young age, the same way that so many kids and adults have been poisoned by what they can now so easily access on their phones. My exposure was long before there were iPhones and Samsungs in every hand, great and small. We lived in Rockford, Illinois at the time, early 1980s, and I remember on late night tv, there was a Canadian comedy show that would air on one of the local channels. The show was called *Bizarre.* I don't remember much about the show other than thinking that the host always had what I would now call a smug look on his face, and this one thing; it seemed that the whole premise of the show was that the star of the show was surrounded by these beautiful women, and he was always trying to verbally trick them into taking their shirts off on camera and flashing everyone. My Dad loved to watch comedy, and I think he stumbled on *Bizarre* somehow. I remember watching it one night, but when one of the women took their top off, my parents quickly turned it off and banned us from watching it ever again.

The cement was poured however, and over many years, it began to set. I recall doing my utmost to sneak in ways to turn on *Bizarre* without any sound and just catch a glimpse, but that was very difficult in the days when a television was a huge device in the center of the living room. I was successful at times, but rarely. In a Christian home, I had few opportunities to feed that side of myself. I loved to see movie posters for fantasy movies and book covers by great artists like Frank Frazetta and Boris Vallejo, with strong heroic men and scantily clad, shapely women. It soon progressed to the days of cable, early HBO and Cinemax late night, and scrambled Playboy channel, that every so often would unscramble as I gazed at it, hoping I might see something.

There were movies with friends at friend's houses when I got to be a teenager, doing what teens often do. Sometimes, we'd pick a movie just based on content. This was all happening alongside the efforts of living a normal kid's life.

A platform was being built in a secret room in my heart and mind. It wasn't until I got to college that the addiction to pornography became a cement that set in my mind, that would later have to be broken. A college friend gave me a tape, presumably because he could probably tell I was pretty naïve and stunted when it came to women and romance, and he told me to watch it. He said I'd enjoy it. I'd never seen anything like it. It was a videotape full of pornography. Oh, if my friend had only realized what he'd done, the doors in my mind that he opened up. Honestly, doors that I opened up. I didn't have to watch the tape. I struggled from then on, sometimes renting porno tapes, and hoping no one I knew would catch me. I was still going to church every Sunday, and I truly did love Jesus. But my platform of secrecy was being built, brick by brick, and almost beginning to overshadow everything else. The guilt was tremendous.

I thought marriage would change that, and Felacia did too. But it seemed to get worse. Now that I could fulfill some of the natural desires that God gave us as a couple, porn addiction was the secret shadow of guilt that hung over our union. That brings us back to the abuser that causes pain to those around them. While I was not the traditional abusive husband in the dirty wifebeater tank top, I had become the secret abuser who was always angry, because I felt guilty that I couldn't be all I needed to be in the bedroom. There was no problem physically. We were both young and healthy. My problem was in the mind. They say pornography alters the very structure of the human mind, and I believe it. The mind has to be rewired back to normalcy after pornography. Pornography became a secret platform that stood between Felacia and I, and I increasingly found it harder and harder to climb over that platform to her. She was always so gracious in those days, even in her own anger and trauma, and she tried to work with me through an issue that I discussed with her before we married. She just didn't know the scope of how bad it was. I don't think I knew either. I assumed marriage would change it since we could have all the sex we wanted. That rewiring didn't happen that way.

I became a mentally and emotionally abusive man. Pornography, as you delve into it, becomes an increasingly abusive medium, heading into depths of depravity that I won't even glorify here. It normalizes abuse of women even at its shallowest depths. But at its deepest point, it normalizes the sexual abuse of children. It's a slippery slope that gets steeper the further you go into it. Now I can never imagine in my darkest dreams ever having any desires toward a child of any age. I think it's insidious. But I do believe the track that pornography inevitably leads to ends at a child. That is a destination I never wanted to find myself, so it became increasingly important to figure out where the root of all this negative sexual energy comes from.

I believe in the depths of my soul that pornography is not rooted in sex or sexual deviancy. I believe it's rooted in power, domination, and anger. These are the triggers that fuel pornography and its widespread use. That is by design, and it always has been. We live in a society that feeds on a select few controlling and using the masses. The methods used feed the lust for power for those in power and feeds the anger of those under them. It's a massive trap, and more and more of us fall headlong into the trap every day. I found out just yesterday that a former co-worker had just been arrested... for viewing child pornography. He was always a quiet, even-tempered guy that I really liked working around. I would never have guessed it of him. He seemed steady and level-headed. I have noticed that the ones that seem to fall often come across that way. I would have been one of them.

What has become my resolve with all of this?

One resolve is not to rest on platforms, even Christianity. Jesus Christ is my Lord and Savior. Every aspect of my life should reflect that. Making a platform to my family and friends and the world is counterproductive because it's so easy to fall off the edge. I must be the man God made me to be, quietly and with great resolution. I don't have to rest on a platform of Blackness. I am a Black man because I accept that definition that society created when it suits me. I can't change my race and I don't want to, but I'm not going to allow it to confine me to a narrow platform of what things constitute being Black. I don't have to rest on a platform of being a good husband. I just need to be a good, honorable man and get to know my best friend, Felacia, as we continue to journey together through the life we have chosen. We're both adults. We don't need each other. We are no longer co-dependent. We want each other. We want to be together. I don't need to show pictures of us smiling and hugging on Facebook and Instagram to prove to anyone that we are happy, because we prove or disprove it every day by the way we act and manage our lives together, and that proof is for us alone. I don't have to rest on a platform of being a good dad, either. I just need to love and connect with my son and my daughter, be real and available to them. If I can do that, I know I'll find them thriving in the places and opportunities Felacia and I envisioned for them, and they will have peace.

My other resolve is that I never make another platform out of my pain. I want to find a way to heal it and make a platform out of the healing. I have always loved the Alcoholics Anonymous model. The alcoholic admits he or she is an alcoholic, and they admit that they need something or someone greater than themselves to overcome it. I have found that I don't want to make a platform out of pornography addiction. That gives it too much power. I don't want to make a platform out of a bad marriage or a successful one. I don't want to make a platform out of my race. I do want to find healing in it, and much of that healing rests in Christ alone for me. And it rests in me as well. Perfect people lean on themselves. Imperfect people lean on God. Jesus is THE platform, a firm foundation I can stand solidly on, to break down that platform of pain.

CHAPTER 6

A MARGINALIZED MAN

Would it be considered an oxymoron to state the opinion that men can be marginalized? And that marginalization of men can create and does create an angry man?

Marginalization has become quite a buzzword in our modern American society, and it is defined by Merriam Webster as such: to relegate to an unimportant or powerless position within a society or group. Just as I wholeheartedly believe about racism, I believe anyone can marginalize anyone else, and that marginalization creates great anger in the person who has been rendered powerless. What often happens is that we as humans tend to decide under what parameters a particular person fits or doesn't fit a certain definition, and if they don't meet the criteria, they are outcast as not being a relevant part of that group. Being an outcast is always going to generate anger in the person who is marginalized. I believe that the most marginalized group by far at any time in any society is children. They usually can't speak up for themselves, and many times, they are not listened to. That is why we have a world full of angry adults; adults are the children who weren't heard. I've talked about different ways that I have been marginalized over the years, especially as a kid, and in so many ways I have marginalized others as well, especially as an adult. Because our purpose here is not a societal commentary, but more an understanding of feelings and emotions related to anger, I will tell two similar stories. As these stories are not my own, we will bring all the chickens home to roost by the end of the chapter.

Both these stories are of guys I have worked with over the years. I was in the power generation industry for 8 years and have been in the oil and gas industry for 15 years and counting. I mentioned in the previous chapter that a former co-worker of mine was recently arrested for child pornography. The previous history in that saga was this: he was a young guy, in his twenties, married only a few years, with maybe one or two kids. During the time I knew him, he and his wife went through a rough divorce. After that time, he continued to work with us, but I rarely saw him at work. I came to work one day and found out he had been fired for being AWOL several times. He just didn't show up to work when he was scheduled to be there. I truly hated to hear that he had been fired, but I knew he had had some issues with his divorce, and we as his former co-workers all gathered that he let himself get fired to get out of paying alimony and child support. I had another co-worker in a different craft, a real aggressive go-getter that everyone knew to be full of energy, but with a bit of an emotional short fuse. This gentleman was known to be a very hard worker, and he worked a tremendous amount of overtime. But there came a point where he began to be AWOL very often as well, and he too ended up getting fired. I recently heard that he worked a lot of overtime when he was with the company, and this was because he had also been recently divorced. The story was that he was paying $3200 a month in alimony and child support and was only bringing home $250 on a two-week paycheck. We make good money in my industry, especially for where we live, but even so, paying out $3200 a month is not sustainable on our salary. So again, this co-worker let himself get fired; his ex would not get alimony, child support or 401k that way.

I am in no way justifying the paths that these two guys chose to take to relieve what I am sure became truly burdensome to them both, but I can imagine the anger and frustration they must have felt. I don't know their whole stories but surely if I had heard the ex-wives' side of things, I might have more context for it all. I do know this; both men felt marginalized. They felt unimportant. They felt their needs and opinions, perhaps even their lives didn't matter. Yes, men can be marginalized just like women, even in a society where men hold a lot of power and women have faced great oppression for centuries on end. Yes, Black people can be racist and marginalize White people in a society where Black people and Brown people and other oppressed peoples have been marginalized for far too long. Because in the end, we're all humans, and all humans have some form of power.

If I can't be considered racist as a Black person if I make a derogatory comment about White people, that means that mentally, physically, intellectually, and spiritually, I am truly less than them as a person, but God Himself made us all equal. If a woman cannot marginalize a man by the way she thinks about and treats the men in her circle, women would have to be considered inferior to men and truly beneath us, and that is in no way true. Women are different from men but are in every way equal in the eyes of God. To be equal means that we can be equally abusive or disdainful of each other. To say that a woman cannot support herself without a man is to say she is inferior, yet some of these financial awards to ex-wives say just that. We as men must also realize that we can't treat our wives and women in general as if they are children. We marginalize them when we do, and I believe women in this situation often feel justified to expect that man to completely take care of them.

One of the traits I greatly admired in Felacia when we were dating was that she was adamant about having her own and taking care of herself. I offered one time when we were dating to pay her phone bill. She vehemently told me "No" and said never to ask her if I could pay any of her bills again. I was impressed and okay with that. Unfortunately, I was the kind of man when we were young married that I have seen more of in recent years: the man that wants a woman to take care of him. I moved to Alabama to be closer to her, and she was graduating school with a nursing degree. By the time we married, she was working as a nurse and beginning to make a good income. My rate of pay was only $10 an hour, not enough to support both of us. I didn't have a checkbook, so I paid bills with money orders. I had a credit card bill that was several hundred dollars that I hadn't paid since college, which was a result of only one purchase when I got the card: an $80 pair of tennis shoes. When I moved to Alabama, I stayed with Felacia's aunt for nearly 9 months until her aunt passed away, and about three months into my stay, I quit my new job at a shipyard because I didn't like welding or getting my hands dirty.

My life plan was to be a teacher and a famous writer, but the potential for $19 an hour and a chance to move from New Orleans to be closer to Felacia all made sense at the time. I was a very sorry excuse for a husband. As an adult, I became a marginalized man, who had been a marginalized kid. I had always felt powerless, and powerless people feel like someone needs to take care of them. In fact, they feel like they owe it to them. I don't think I believed that Felacia owed me anything. But

I did believe, in the baser parts of me, that since she had it, she might as well give what she had to me. We had an argument one particular time when I was staying with her aunt. I was so tremendously irresponsible then. I was not buying my own groceries when I stayed with her aunt, and I was not paying rent, even though she was gracious enough to let me live with her while I was dating her niece. Felacia was so embarrassed when her aunt complained to her that I was going in the cabinets and eating whatever I found there. Felacia confronted me about it, and my angry response was that I had been watching those particular items of food for weeks, and nobody was eating them, so I figured I could eat them. Trifling! In my immaturity, I got angry when she asked me why in any sense of logic would I think eating food I didn't purchase would be okay? I totally didn't see the problem.

There is truly a problem that arises when a person doesn't realize the innate power that God has given to them. They stop trying. There was a very triggering episode of Marvel's "The Falcon and the Winter Soldier" where a Black former super-soldier, who had the same powers garnered the same way as Captain America, was living years later in poverty and obscurity somewhere in a large city. The Falcon went to find this super-soldier who still retained the powers he once had but had gained a bitterness that had rendered him powerless. He complained to the Falcon that the scientists who created him subjected him to 30 years of brutal experiments, and that he as a hero was never recognized for his achievements. I remember feeling very put-off by that episode and the ideas it purported for this reason. While it seemed like the episode meant for us to feel sorry for this man, it actually made me feel more like the man was sorry. If I had the powers of Captain America, there is no way that I would spend 30 years allowing someone to just experiment on me without trying to find some way to escape it! This was a man with great power but without the resolve to use it. I have resolved not to marginalize myself like this man did for 30 years.

I believe that herein lies the problem, and herein is where anger is generated; when we allow ourselves to be marginalized, when we allow ourselves to be powerless, we determine that another person is superior to us, and thus we have no recourse in our situation. There was a point early in our marriage where Felacia had had enough. She was ready for a divorce. She was going to take the kids and get an apartment near a local public school and let me keep the house. I asked her, "Well, what am I going to do?" She made the bulk of the money. She paid all the bills. She bought our groceries. She arranged sitters for the kids when we both had to work. She did everything other than go to the power plant to work in my place. Yet, I expected her to figure out how to make my life work if she left. My intention was never to aggrieve her in that way; it's just how I was wired at the time. I am glad to say that as of now, she's been a housewife for the past seven years, and we both live off my paycheck. She worked for seventeen years in a very thankless and harsh profession, and I am proud that God has blessed me to be able to take her out of that life. Nonetheless, as a housewife, especially a Black one, she has sometimes been marginalized because she doesn't work, especially since both the kids are practically adults. We had a friend of ours recently, a very successful Black woman careerwise, say she felt like as a Black woman, it was an automatic certainty that she'd always have to work. And this is more of a notion when the husband is Black.

These ideas are all just that... ideas. Notions. They are not truths or facts or inevitabilities. Yet we treat them as such. That is why I believe marginalization begins in the mind, and why I think it makes us all so angry to be marginalized. I as a Black husband can support my wife financially. And my wife could support herself if we were not together or if I passed away. Women don't need men to support them, nor do they need their husbands to be their fathers. Men don't need to assume that upon divorce they are wholly financially responsible for that ex-wife, nor should she or the U.S. Court system assume that either. Financially successful women shouldn't assume that a man with a good job who makes less than them is less than them because of it. There are great men who don't own the business who would make excellent husbands for women who do.

Empowerment starts in the mind as much as marginalization does. I saw myself as marginalized when I married Felacia, and I stayed in a mindset that marginalized me for a long time. Anytime she would say how she did all the bills, or how she paid for everything at our wedding, I got angry and claimed she was bragging. I absolutely hated to hear that. But these days, I am very proud of her and her sacrifices to help us become a family back then. Now would I recommend a young woman do that in the attempt to marry a young man? Absolutely not. While I am very proud to take care of and support her financially now, I wish with all my heart that I would have started off as a young husband with a different mindset about taking care of her.

I do believe however, that a young woman should also realize it is unfair to go into a marriage with the sole aim of finding a man, young or old, to take care of her. Nor should a young man go into a marriage or relationship with the aim that that woman will take care of him while he lays around and plays video games all day. They are both contributors to the life they choose to live together. And a person who contributes should never feel marginalized.

CHAPTER 7

ADJUSTING THE VOLUME

Have you ever met a person whose presence seems to fill a room? This person enters a space and who they are seems to expand until it permeates every corner of any place they enter. We've all met those people at a dinner party or gathering. Their laugh is the loudest and most unique. Their stories are the funniest or the most poignant. Their style is the sharpest. That sort of person can fill a room in a good way or a bad way. I generally tend to think of people who are that way in a good way. My Dad was that way. He had a joyful laugh and a booming voice, a voice trained by Loyola University to sing opera, though he never continued in that vein professionally. Dad was boisterous and a lot of fun to be around. Mom was steady and gentle and calm, and I tend to be much more like her. But Felacia has always reminded me of my Dad in the way she seemed to fill a room. Her laugh would sound way across a large building, and I always knew it was her laughing. Her hospitality has always been larger-than-life. Where I would probably invite guests over and we'd order some pizzas, she'd be making her famous red beans and rice, going out to grab some Champy's Chicken, and baking a key lime cake with cream cheese icing on it. If a neighbor has a death in the family, I'm sending my regards by text, but she's ordering flowers from us. Back when Felacia was nursing, she even sat up all night with a pregnant neighbor at that neighbor's house when she was having some pregnancy woes. That's just the kind of person she is.

Felacia is a woman of tremendous volume, with a wonderful ability to care for and seek to meet needs. She always makes herself responsible, even when she isn't responsible. I, on the other hand, am her complete opposite, and might have at one time been considered her archnemesis. I do not in any way feel responsible or take responsibility for things that are not mine to do. Now I can be tremendously empathetic, feeling deeply the emotions of a person who's going through tough times. I am a master of indignancy. I will rail and rue the misfortune with that person, feeling their pain alongside them. But at the end of the day, I don't feel responsible to fix it. Felacia feels responsible for fixing it. This can be an overwhelmingly weighty trait for a person of great volume to have, because they often exhaust themselves trying to fix everything for everyone.

Thus, for many years of our marriage, I was always in some way trying to turn her volume down. She has said to me that sometimes she has felt like she is too much for some people. She would drop everything to help, but the rare times that she would let down her façade of having it all together, no one seemed to be there to hold her arms up. Including me. She's the type of person that seems to always have it all together, so she often inadvertently gives off the impression that she doesn't need help. She'll get in there and get her hands dirty trying to make things right. I believe that is one of the many beautiful things about her, yet I often found myself angry at her for those very same traits. I applauded her in her continued efforts to help and do good, until it required something of <u>me</u>. Then I'd get angry and tell her she was taking on too much, inconveniencing me in some way. I didn't realize that often in her efforts to help, she felt pressure from others that shouldn't have been hers to feel, so the added pressure from my side of things nearly broke her. I thought she loved the requests and the constant phone calls for advice or support or need, so I'd only complain if I felt it infringed in any way on me or my time. I was a poor protector. She didn't love those things; she felt obligated to do them oftentimes.

I had never gotten into her shoes to realize the volume that I thought was there was not actually there. Cinderella really did have small feet and needed smaller shoes. And like Cinderella, there can be family pressures brought to bear that become very heavy and burdensome, making those who tend to take responsibility end up bearing the weight of things and situations they're not equipped for. The volume for that overachiever needs to be turned down. I will never forget when our volume was turned down, quite abruptly. I will explain why I say <u>our</u> volume in a minute. It was 2017, around the holidays at the end of a year with some major life changes for us, especially in the realm of employment. We decided a few months before that the nurse with a purse needed to retire, and so Felacia came off her job. We lived off just my income from that time and have for almost seven years since, by God's grace. While both she and I assumed the transition would be simple and easy, neither of us took into account how life would be for a woman who had always taken responsibility, who had made things happen from our wedding day until that point when we decided to retire her, to just come home and be a housewife. The transition was not smooth, it was not simple, it was not easy, and it was not pretty. The first few months, it seemed like we argued all the time. I believe now that we were finally airing out a lot of things that we just didn't have time to discuss before. We were always too busy. I often complained when we were both working that when we did get around to having a dinner date together, we always had to hash out the hard stuff. I dreaded dinner dates for that reason.

So, we had been several months in our changing roles, she as house-wife and I as sole provider. There was a day when we'd had another argument, so I left the house. I had determined to go see one of the new Star Wars films that was being released around that time. Felacia texted me as I was on my way down the road that some family was coming to visit, and of course I was glad to be gone because I didn't feel like pretending to be nice. A few minutes later, Felacia texted me that something happened at the house and to please come home. Which I immediately did, under the circumstances. As it turns out, my sweet wife had gotten backed into a corner once again in her efforts to try to fix and balance things, but this time, the consequences were a lot heavier than usual. I felt terrible. I should have been there, been there for her. Honestly, I should have been there for us. That is the essence of why I said earlier that I had to turn *our* volume down. The volume of things in our lives was ours, not just hers. I had always seen the volume of responsibilities and obligations as hers, as things she took on when she should have said "no", when she should have ignored the call or the text because it wasn't hers to do, as Suzanne Stabile would say. I didn't see what she took on as being mine too. I was a poor gatekeeper.

I know now that one of the best things we ever did for our marriage was for Felacia to come home, in so many ways. I needed the experience of being responsible, of carrying the weight and volume of my family, of leaning on God when I didn't have an answer. I expected my poor young wife to have the answers, and in the case of feeling obligated, to stop asking questions. She felt like she should be helping more, and when she made even the slightest effort, her help was expected. So she helps. And I'd get mad at her for being suckered into cushioning things for the able-bodied, the ones God said could help themselves. I have had to resolve that what Felacia takes on becomes mine, and what I take on becomes hers, and all that that means. Which means I have to speak up and intervene when I feel like she is getting into something she might later find overwhelming, instead of showering her with I-told-you-so's when she begins to feel spent, or getting angry at her for committing to something that overwhelms her. I have to be willing to get my hands dirty, be ready to make the call even if I'm seen as mean or selfish or unwilling to help, if I can protect her peace in any way. I was always good at protecting my own peace. I am truly an enneagram 9. But my Felacia is truly an enneagram 2, and she often rushes in to help. Fools may rush in at times, but only an emotional sadist would allow them to do so. I began to take her on as mine, as my responsibility, and so I began to take on her needs and her struggles as mine too. She has told me that these seven years of housewifery have been the most restful and peaceful since her days living in her apartment alone in college. That has and will continue to make me very happy. My prayer of late has been that she finds out what she really wants, for herself, and not for anyone else. That is truly a challenge for a person whose life goals have always centered around others. She is meeting the challenge splendidly.

Felacia and I were talking to a friend of hers one time when her friend stated, "Joel, Felacia is a handful!" I replied, "It's a good thing I have big hands!" And it truly is a good thing. As we're learning to adjust our volume together, she is slowly becoming less stressed and overwhelmed, and I am slowly becoming less uptight and angry. That's one of the many problems in our world, creating stress, up-tightness, and chaos in our minds. This world is so noisy. It seems like the parasitic hold of our iPhones and the constant cacophony of Unsocial Media are a constant noise not only in our ears, but in our minds. Gone are the days when a phone call was met by the barriers of time and presence. If we weren't at home, there was no phone to answer. If the hour was late, the phone could be disabled. There was no Facebook to check, no Instagram to post to, no TikTok tic-tocking repeatedly in our minds, "Look at me, look at me, Look at me..." Our hands have to be more than just a flick of the thumb, scrolling mindlessly through life. That's why I've got big hands, made to support myself and my family by working and producing, made to clap and celebrate our victories and soothe with a gentle pat after our failures. I believe those big hands have a big task these days: covering my ears and Felacia's ears at key times, helping us block out all the noise, turn down the volume, so we can hear what God is saying to us. As I have said, God is never going to shout over us, nor is He going to shout over the volume of this noisy, chaotic world. We must adjust the volume to hear His voice; our willingness to adjust tells Him that we are listening, because He is always speaking. And His voice is beautiful.

CHAPTER 8

A NICE GUY AND A KIND BAR

"Nice tells you what you want to hear, but **kind** is honest."

God has a way of speaking through anything, even a KIND bar commercial. I had never heard of the KIND brand, a snack bar company that purports to be kind to its customers by the sort of natural ingredients they use to make their products, but when their ad came on TV, something about what it said struck me, and I never forgot it. I was in one of those many occasions in my personal journey wherein I was asking God quite often what was wrong with me. Why was I so tired and so angry all the time? This was a period where I was listening closely, trying to understand why my many attempts not to go off the deep end were failing, and something about that simple slogan arrested me right in the middle of what I was doing.

I had always assumed that nice people were automatically kind people. Nice people were the kind of people I wanted to associate myself with, known amongst friends and peers as steady, even-tempered, loyal, good-natured, upstanding. Nice guys hold the door open for women. They help old ladies cross busy streets. They stop to help stranded motorists push a crippled car off to the side of the road. Nice guys. A Christian guy should be a nice guy and be known as a nice guy, at least in my opinion. Being a moral boy scout was a part of the code of what constitutes a good man. I would have been the guy who would have told you what you wanted to hear, because what you needed to hear might have been a hard pill to swallow. I had no inkling that kindness and niceness were in no way twin brothers. In fact, niceness and kindness might even be polar ends of the same spectrum.

I, for example, in being what I considered a nice guy, would connect with friends and interact with them on a superficial level, but with my perpetual undercurrent of anger, I would quickly write off people in my temporary circle of friendship if in some way they disappointed me. It wasn't always an immediate ghosting... often it was just a gradual backing away from them, almost a fade away. At the time of this KIND bar epiphany, I was very, very cognizant of how poorly skilled I was at friendship. So you can only imagine being married to me. I wasn't very kind. During this period, Felacia and I had made a new friendship with another couple at our stage of life who were a part of the circle of families in our town. Both Felacia and I were seeking to develop richer friendships, so we connected with this couple, and began to hang out with them regularly. On our first major outing, they invited us to spend the day on a particular recreational activity with them, and as it turns out, this particular activity requires a fair degree of expense to engage in. Having been invited to join them, it didn't occur to me at the time to offer to supplement fuel costs. Felacia, sweet and generous as always, brought snacks to augment the ones they already had. But somehow, as the outing progressed, it was as if we, by being there, were becoming burdensome to the outing, and I think both they and we were ready to call it a day by the end.

As Felacia and I always do, we took some time on the drive home to process how we felt about everything. There had been some relational damage in our lives at the time, with people outside of ourselves, so getting back into the fray of friendship was a tender endeavor, like stepping into salt water with a cut on your leg. I, as I was wont to do, decided I didn't like the husband all that much and was content to leave the relationship alone. But we both knew this was a good family as good families go, and not everyone is on their game all the time. Felacia suggested that I volunteer a decent sum of cash from us after the fact, towards the outing we had just taken, and after a bit of begrudging thought, I quickly realized that was a brilliant idea. It just made sense. Not only would we feel like we contributed to the outing in a tangible way, but for us, it would show good faith that we weren't there trying to be friendship gold-diggers, just there for what we could get out of the relationship. What Felacia suggested that we do was to perform an act of kindness. It was very satisfying to feel as if I vindicated the people that I believed the couple saw us to be by choosing to be the people we showed them.

The incident reminds me of a time when I was perhaps 6 or 7 years old. We went for a weekend to visit with some new friends in Arkansas, who had a beautiful cabin up in the mountains. I don't remember much about the visit, but I remember the couple we visited had a son who was a few years younger than me. For whatever reason, he didn't want me to play with any of his toys. He wasn't an only child, but his older brother and sister were of the ages where they had families of their own, so he was basically the only child of much older parents. As I remember, he was a bratty kid at that age, and his parents kept apologizing for him the whole visit. Finally, I think my Dad could tell the whole visit was bothering me, and on one of our days there, we took a family trip to the local mall in a town near where they lived. I recall complaining to my Dad that I wasn't having much fun when he asked me if I was enjoying myself, and I told him why. Of course, as a man of deep feeling, it bothered him. He suggested something that I have remembered from then until now.

"Let's buy him a toy. How about this nice truck?"

I was flabbergasted. Why in heaven's name would I buy another toy for this kid whose room was chock full of toys, far more than I would have dreamed of at the time? Especially when he was being mean to me? To my young mind, that made absolutely no sense. The toy truck was exactly the one I would have picked for myself. Dad went on to explain that he learned to do that when he was a little kid from one of the adults in his life. When someone is being mean or ugly to you, try doing something kind for them and see how you feel. I was tremendously skeptical that it would make me feel any better, and I really wanted the toy truck for myself, but at that point, I was willing to try anything to make that kid be nicer. So we bought the truck, brought it home, and presented it to him with his parents standing right there. As I remember, Dad gave the truck to me to present to him, which I did. His parents seemed to be very grateful, almost a bit ashamed about his previous behavior, and even the young kid seemed to soften for the remainder of the time we were there. To my young, impressionable mind, something about the act of kindness itself was exceptionally satisfying and soothing to a troubled mind, as if in passing the truck over to my young friend I also passed any anger or remembrance of the negative past between us out of my hands. All that didn't matter anymore. I don't know if he changed any after I left, but I knew I had changed. Kindness felt foreign, but it felt good.

The joy of kindness had become foreign to me again as an adult. I had long replaced it with being nice, trying always to appear pleasant and agreeable. Kindness involves generosity and consideration for others. I believe being nice ultimately can become a bit of a selfish endeavor. In pursuit of my own peace, I wanted to appear nice to those around me. In both instances, these two different families were kind enough to invite our family, whether it was under my Mom and Dad or under the family Felacia and I had created, to be a part of their world for a time. And I entered both worlds as someone receiving. Only in the giving did I find myself becoming a part of the world I found myself in. That is perhaps why I personally believe while a kind person cannot consistently be an angry person, a nice person can consistently and deeply remain an angry person. A kind person may give advice to a friend they care about, even if they know it may not be taken well, because they care about that friend. That care for their friend is a gift they give. The nice person, in the interests of self-preservation, will reserve the advice because they don't want to offend, but instead they allow that friend to fall into harm. I have resolved that I will always endeavor to truly be kind, which can often involve being vulnerable as you care for those around you.

As I have explored this resolve to be kind, I've also had to come to terms with the fact that not everyone will be good for that kindness. There is a lot of talk in our current culture about toxic people, so much so that the term has become a buzzword and even lost a bit of its potency. The old saying goes that we should kill 'em with kindness, but some people you can't kill with kindness because they are already dead. Our world is full of toxic people. Our world is full of narcissists. My general approach has been to prepare myself emotionally and mentally to deal with the toxic people. The massive problem with that approach is that I have tended to regard everyone as potentially toxic and will often tend to either avoid people or try to please them. In either regard, I usually fail. There is a genuineness in kindness, a lack of pretense, that niceness just cannot emulate, and it is from this kindness that emotional endurance comes. When I am honest with myself, I'm a lot less angry with myself and with others. When I am kind, I'm a lot less angry, and I can be honest with others when necessary. Thus, my better approach has been to meet the challenge of not being a toxic person.

As it turns out, the friends we had the outing with remained friends of ours for quite a while, three to four years perhaps, and all the while both Felacia and I determined to do our best to be gracious friends to them, as we hoped they would be to us. I knew a testing ground of my emotional maturity would be whether I would write my friend off or whether I would give the friendship a chance. Only afterwards would I allow myself to decide perhaps the friendship wasn't for me. I can honestly say in this instance, I truly did everything I could to try to build a genuine friendship with this particular guy. What finally sealed the deal for me and allowed me to be okay with letting it go was this: my friend wasn't particularly kind in several tangible ways, and it began to feel quite harmful to pursue the friendship. One of the last times I remember us getting together was at a big party at their house. As always, amongst the large group of people that they knew as friends, but we were just getting to know, we were the only Black couple. Felacia and I don't generally make that an issue for us. We just like hanging out with good people. The problem was that the party was as usual a dance party, and the music of choice was hip-hop, and the hip-hop of choice was rife with the n-word, as certain types of hip-hop are. I as a Black man have had some negative run-ins with that word over the years so it's a word that I keep way out of my vocabulary. My friend on the other hand, seems to find it cool to gather with a group of other adults over food and some drinks, and dance to some "fun" music. Somehow as Felacia and I sat amongst the various clusters of people, mingling about, I began to feel that it was deeply unkind to play something like that when you're in racially mixed company down in a small town in the Deep South. This wasn't the first time something awkward like this had happened with these friends, and I assure you, there was no intentional malice. They just weren't thinking. As I've resolved to be kind, I've had to resolve to think. Think about the people I'm around. Think about my assumptions, my stereotypes.

We recently attended another gathering with the completely opposite demographic; nearly every family there was Black, and there was one White family who were visiting the area but were soon to be moving to the US permanently from their native home in a European country. As we were playing a board game, the game had several questions related to a sordid and terrible period in the history of their native country and the world at large, and the conversation became quite awkward as they told us all how they were treated during a government intake interview when being asked their intentions in moving to the US. We could all tell they were deeply hurt and affected by how they and their young son were treated, though I am quite sure the officials doing the questioning were only doing their jobs. Again, the malice felt was not intentional. Our lack of kindness is never intentional, nor is it confined to any one race, gender, nationality, social status or financial level. We all struggle to be kind.

The road to becoming a toxic person is when we choose not to struggle to be kind and decide just to be nice, and we become further

and further detached from those around us. I have resolved that for
me, the struggle is real, but it is also necessary. I wrote a poem in 1997
called "Nice People", and I think it is worth sharing here:

NICE PEOPLE

I work with nice people.
*

Aybeeceedee always tells me
When they are going to V-Mart
On lunch break, in case I want
Her to bring me an order of lasagna.
She shares her fruit punch with
Me when she brings her gallon jug.

She dislikes our 300+ pound
Coworker, and calls her "Big Momma"
When she's not around.

Aybeeceedee is nice.
*

John Doe took me out to lunch
At D's on Fr. Street when I
First started working. He paid.
We talked about movies in passing
During the work day; Kubrick,
The Italian Eastwood pictures.
I enjoy discussing films with him.

He strongly dislikes the young lady
In charge of the front desk. Said
She's a real "B—ch!"

I like him, too. John Doe is nice.
*

Eckswhyzee always says hello
When we see each other. She has
A quick, sharp sense of humor
That I admire. She spoke well
Of me to my wonderful former
Boss when they saw each other.

She strongly dislikes a lot of people.
Her pet name for John Doe is "a—hole".

I like her. If you met her,
You'd think she was very nice.
*

*

*

I wonder if being called
"Nice" is really a compliment .

CHAPTER 9

THE MAN CHILD

The 1980's were an amazing time to be a kid. Our bikes had banana seats with vibrant oranges, reds, yellows and blues, and the designs had little to do with function and a lot to do with style. And the Big Wheel was the coolest trike ever invented. The '80s were the heyday of action figures. I personally loved G.I. Joe. I had a lot of the action figures from that era of G.I. Joe, like Flint, Duke, Sgt. Slaughter, Gung Ho.... My all-time favorites were Storm Shadow and Snake Eyes. Of course, I had to have their counterparts Cobra Commander, Destro, Tomax and Xamot. I had the original X-19 Stealth fighter, the Cobra HISS tank, and my forever favorite the Skystriker XP-14F with Ace as the pilot. Transformers was a big hit. M.A.S.K. Brave Starr. After-school cartoons like Silverhawks, Inspector Gadget, Voltron, and Mr. T had me rushing home to turn on the TV. The cartoon theme songs were the best in the '80s. The sitcom themes of the 80s were the best of all time for that matter. Gimme A Break. The Cosby Show. Family Ties. Family Matters!

I remember so many great children's movies like Explorers, The Neverending Story, The Dark Crystal, Flight of the Navigator... there were so many good movies and tv shows during that time that I'd need a whole chapter of this book just to reminisce on them all. To my generation, the '80s was probably the heyday of entertainment and the singular era where consumerism meshed with the fantastic need of Americans for escapism. My friend Scott and I would often hang out at his house or mine after church on Sundays, and I'd bring all my G.I. Joe figures and vehicles, and we'd have three- or four-hour epic battles starring our G.I. Joe figures on the stairway or the living room floor, until nearly every action figure had bravely died in battle. If we went to Scott's house, we would without fail have sloppy joes for Sunday dinner before starting the day's adventure. Those were pivotal, amazing times, with neither Scott nor I realizing that they were. Scott was an awkward kid, a thin, pale White kid with a special dandruff disorder that left him with a constant dusting of dandruff flakes on his shoulders. He explained to me exhaustively what the condition was that caused his excessive dandruff, explaining it in the way a kid does when he doesn't want to be picked on about it. His condition didn't bother me because who I was didn't seem to bother him. I was a chubby Black kid who liked cartoons instead of sports and loved to lay in my room in the summer with a good book, so in a way we were both outcasts.

Being an outcast was one of the greatest themes of a good 80s kids movie. One of the all-time best movies from the 80s about being children on the outside was *Stand By Me*. A group of boys united to go see the fabled body of another kid who was supposedly hit by a train, his dead body still said to be laying in the woods where he'd been struck. Each of the boys in *Stand By Me* had their own sad tale, tales that knit them together by the end of their journey. By film's end, they all returned stronger for it. Feeling like an outcast is always very alienating; feeling like someone else understood and identified with how that felt was always liberating. Though neither Scott nor I were ever considered "cool" amongst our peers, there was a sense of the cool, the "It" factor, in hanging out with another kid who had an innate ability to dream and imagine. Scott was and remains one of the cool kids that I won't forget. Years later, I heard that Scott died, and I was in my early to mid-thirties then, so I know he died young. RIP my young friend.

I often wonder if Scott struggled like I did as a young adult, a young man trying to adjust to being an adult and all that that means. I wrote in a previous chapter about something that Felacia said to me recently that was so profound, and it bears repeating again here: "It's not good to just be a dreamer because that means you are always asleep". This sleep is not a literal sleep; it's more like sleepily stumbling through life, almost sleepwalking. Life is a dream, but you're not living it. I think about some of the pivotal periods of my life since college and on into marriage and fatherhood and career. There are vast swathes of it that I don't remember! I was handling the things I needed to handle, or ignoring them altogether, but I was not living. Occasionally, I'd surface back into reality in some form, but I would inescapably slip back into the dream. One variable that was always consistent: times that I do recall coming out of the dream, my clarity at the time was usually because I was angry about something.

The ability to slip off into a dream at times when your life requires you to be fully awake is what I call the Man-Child Syndrome. There has always been the proverbial man who lives in his mother's basement, the slovenly, unkempt guy with the scraggly neckbeard who sits in his mom's basement playing video games and never goes on dates, emerging into the light only to meet the pizza guy at the door if Mom isn't home. This guy has retreated from people, from life, and only lives in his fantasy world. And deep down, he's always angry. He feels mistreated.

Some years ago, I worked with a man who always smelled of cat hair, and he shuffled around doing odd jobs at our place of work. That place of employment was one in which everyone at the time started at entry level, but the unspoken expectation was that you as an employee would move up in position after a few years. This gentleman was in his late fifties at the time, nearing retirement age, but he had been in that entry level position, sweeping the floors in the machine shop and changing out trash bags, for nearly 35 years. It was said that he was rejected by a woman he tried to court as a young man, and that affected him so much that he lived unmarried with his mother from then on. He would, when asked, do a spot-on imitation of Elvis Presley, but I was warned never to make fun of him or laugh at him if I asked him to do it. He couldn't take the ridicule. I remember wondering how angry at the world he must have been to just give up on life like that. Yet I believe a lot of people just want to retreat into a life without judgement. I imagine he was one of them.

I couldn't judge him because in many ways I was a lot like him. Even though I was married, life was a bit of a dream that I was ambling through, occasionally coming up for air, but with little direction. A symptom of the Man-Child way of life is to find yourself coasting on either highs or lows, cranking along like the two men on the railroad handcar, pumping the lever up and down, a true emotional roller-coaster. I'm happy in my happy place, eating a good meal, gaming, watching a movie. I never want to leave that place. I may drag myself out of that solitary place to meet a need but only long enough to handle whatever real life requires quickly, so I can return to my escape. It's an effort not to live in the real world, where there is pain and loss and tension. These emotions are all too real, and some of us choose not to address them as adults, to receive them as they are. It is a blessing to retain child-like joy in adulthood; I believe it keeps us connected to very real emotions that we need. Retaining childishness, however, only stunts the growth of healthy emotions and replaces them with reactions to stress and pain and sadness that are expressed in the ways a child would express them. Children react as they do because they don't know any differently. Adults should react with maturity because they don't know any less. I have resolved to address sadness as what it is: sadness. Disappointment as disappointment. Loss as loss. Anger as anger. There is something about addressing an emotion on its own terms that brings a true healing to the soul. This was a practice I would not begin to work at for many, many years.

My Dad died in 2005, three weeks after Hurricane Katrina. My brother Nathan died in 2008 at the age of 32 while driving to work one morning. The years between 2005-2010 were very dark for me personally in many ways, but I can honestly say that all the sadness and loss were not addressed for what they truly were. I addressed them as I had learned to address any hard emotion: with anger. I became a deeply angry and pretty morbid man, to the point that I even began to be fascinated with autopsies and death scene photos... all results of a fear of losing someone else I loved and cared about, especially Felacia or our children. The strange thing was, amid the fear and grief, I was also neglecting my family and was very angry at the world. Emotionally, I was very much a child, and managing my feelings like a child. Temper tantrums are not the sole property of children. We adults are very good at them too, and we are finding more and more excuses to allow ourselves to have them. The bullied often become the bullies, and the cycle perpetuates.

I remember a time when I was gaming a lot. I mean I was gaming so much that I was playing for hours at a stretch whenever I wasn't at work, sometimes staying up until 3 or 4 A.M. At this specific time, I was hooked on Skyrim on the PlayStation 4. I'd probably logged several hundred hours playing the main story and wandering off on side missions. My son is an avid gamer himself, and back at that time, he was really starting to get into gaming. He was probably 12 at the time, and I would allow him some hours in the day on weekends to play games he liked. He and his sister liked playing some of the Lego games together. Finally, during my Skyrim era, I allowed him to make his own character on Skyrim since he really wanted to play it. One day, he sheepishly had to reveal to me that he accidentally deleted my Skyrim profile while he was trying to load his. I was so furious that I railed at him about not being careful and just being all-around careless by losing all my hours of work "playing" a video game. I was a true man-child, where my escapism had become more important than my family. My son is a wonderful young man, very sincere and even tempered, but he feels life very deeply, in its good and its bad. My reaction hurt him deep down, but I was so angry, I overlooked how he was probably seeing me just then. I don't believe he wanted to play Skyrim for a long time after that.

The true danger of living an adult life with the emotions of a child is that we begin to stay in the dream world, a world of fantasy, with happy endings and endless do-overs, a world of resets experienced in a world of finality. Real life is in no way like a video game. There are very few do-overs. Idle words and actions cannot be reset in the real world, and some mistakes cannot be rescinded. They can only be amended. I in my adulthood have continued to dream, but also seek to know. I want to know my heart and emotions. I want to know the hearts and needs of the people I love and care about. I want my dreams and goals to include them alongside me. These are the things I seek to know. And as the Joes would always say at the end of each episode of G.I. Joe, "Knowing is half the battle".

CHAPTER 10

A HIDDEN SCAR

My scar used to be really embarrassing. I have a keloid on the back of my head that always made me very self-conscious. I created some scalp issues with poor head shaving in my younger years, and it developed into a prominent scar on the back of my already big head. The scar used to poke out quite prominently until a good dermatologist in our area managed to reduce it to where it is much less noticeable now. At one time, I was embarrassed for anyone to sit behind me in church or at a meeting, or for little kids, who are always curious, to ask about it. The embarrassment was very irrational as I think back on it. People have scars and ailments and syndromes and disabilities that they live with all the time, and many of them don't let themselves be defined by those things. Just as I had to accept the fact that I had an obvious scar on the back of my head, I had to learn to be ok with being Black. Now I'm proud of my skin color. I don't have to put anyone else's skin color down to be proud of my own. I'm proud of my big head. It holds a big brain that allows me to write. I'm proud of my White-sounding voice and diction. I can't change them but I don't have to be embarrassed of them. I've learned to be proud of my scars, physical, emotional, relational, and spiritual. They remind me of how far I've come, in fact how far God has brought me in this life. It is far easier to let your scars be seen, as long as you don't let them define you.

That's the strange thing about scars. They are often results of things you cannot help, like skin color, ethnicity, gender, financial status, social status, country of origin, and even accidents or physical ailments you may have been born with. It is far easier to live life with an awareness that you are given the traits and lot in life you were given without your consent when you are born; whatever scars or beauty you derive after you are born eventually become yours alone. There are some scars however, that come not as a result of an unforeseen injury, but from the unseen choices of people you never met. 2020 was that sort of scar. In many ways, it was a scar on the whole world, and the world has not been the same since. In the years since 2020, I have learned to exercise a new freedom that has helped to reduce my anger at the world tremendously. I chose not to get vaccinated for C-19, and I remain so to this day. How is it possible that this made me less angry, especially with all the gross and obvious atrocities that happened during that time and continue even now?

Choosing not to get vaccinated was one of the first times that I was so convinced of what I believed that no amount of threatening, embarrassing, gaslighting, or cajoling could convince me otherwise. I have strongly held many opinions and beliefs over the years, and many I kept to myself for fear of social excommunication. But in the public attempt by the leaders of the "free" world to railroad all of us "useless eaters", there was a desperateness in their efforts to get us to buy in that didn't ring true. I know many people in my community who got vaccinated merely for threat of losing their livelihood. I know people who lived with C-19 during 2020 and only died AFTER they were admitted to the hospital. I can remember several notable people saying those of us who chose not to get vaccinated didn't deserve to live or should leave our country. For a while, "unvaccinated" was almost like saying "nigger", and with the same disgust. It got that bad for a while. Making that choice became a scar, a hidden one, that those who used their God-given right to choose what to do with the bodies God gave them began to be judged and vilified for.

This was new to me, being rejected for something people could not see. I'd grown used to the rejection for the obvious things. If I walk into a room, I can always be judged on what people see before them. But this was different. No one knew I was unvaccinated unless I told them. It was as if we were a world playing a vast game of poker, and no one wanted to show their hand for fear of what others would think of them. "Did you get the vax?" "Why didn't you get it?" We all wondered as we reemerged into the world after the quarantine was lifted if we'd ever be able to be around each other again. Seeing people's faces and smiles was a joy, without having to wonder what emotional reads we were missing under the masks. Hugs became mandatory for many, while others remained fearful, wearing the masks for many months after the mandates were removed. Some of the gloating was from the vaxxed, some of the gloating was from the unvaxxed. A lot of the true hearts of people, good and bad, showed themselves as we all began to come back out into the light. The angels were mingling with the cockroaches.

I found a lot to be angry about during C-19. When early in the pandemic, the powers that be stated that Black people would be the most susceptible to C-19, I knew the whole thing was suspect. Disease has no genuine sense of race as we know race to be. The fearmongering from then until now was diabolical and cost the lives of many innocent people, many of them very young. A whole generation entered their first year of college in 2020 on lockdown. A whole set of little eyes coupled with little minds were trying to read the lips of fearful parents, wanting to say their first words but hampered by coverings over their parents' mouths. We common folks were not allowed to see scared, aging, dying parents in cold, empty hospitals because the elderly didn't deserve to die in the presence of family members, holding their feeble hands and releasing them on to Glory. Don't you all know there's a pandemic to curb? It was such a vast pandemic in fact that many of the rich and famous were able to come and go as usual, unhindered by anything on their faces or on their consciences. It was a terrible time.

It was a terrible time indeed. It was an angry time. It was a tremendously sad time. But somehow, even in the midst of all this loss, even now there remains a hope. Genesis 50:20 says this: "But as for you, ye thought evil against me; *but* God meant it unto good, to bring to pass, as *it is* this day, to save much people alive". To paraphrase this very hopeful Bible verse, what the enemy meant for evil, God meant for good, to save a lot of people. The events of 2020 were the evil results of evil plans for evil times. That much is true. It is infuriating to realize that much of what happened was not happenstance and was in fact the plan all along. The positive in this is the knowledge that 2020 has happened many, many times before, but very few of us were awake to that fact. When Joseph made the statement about his brothers in Genesis 50:20, he stated that truth in full awareness of the evil that his brothers, his kin, and his family had done to him. That position of man to man is no different now. The sins committed from one to the other on this earth are committed brother against brother, sister against sister. Times have not changed from the time of Joseph until now. Times have not changed from the time of Jesus Christ until now. Men still crucify you because you think differently. Men still crucify you for thinking for yourself. Men crucify you for not taking a vaccine. Men crucify you for taking a vaccine. I've heard so many "serves them right"s from some of the bitter unvaccinated when they hear of those with vaccine injuries, even saying those poor people deserve what they got for getting the shot. I wish there was an injection of kindness, of mercy, of grace for suffering people, no matter what choices they make. Those who live in a world of revenge and vindictiveness may find that their virus is much deeper and more incurable than a mere respiratory bug. They have a heart disease, and not a physical one.

The joy I find in these trying times is this: the same healing I find in being able to confidently choose what not to put in my body is the same healing I find in being able to confidently choose what not to put in my mind and my heart. Why live the healthy life I seek by my choice in one area but allow my spirit to be poisoned by anger? I hope and pray that all people, vaccinated and unvaccinated, are able to live the quality of life and the length of life they choose to live. Every day on this earth is a gift; sometimes it takes someone trying to take that gift away for us to begin to live life to its fullest. Joseph had scars of shame: thrown into a pit, thrown into jail, nearly thrown into the arms of his master's wife. But all his scars led him to become the second in command of all Egypt, where he began to live that full and rich life he dreamed of. Perhaps our scars can do the same for us, give us a constant reminder of where we have come from, and where we want to go.

CHAPTER 11

THE COMFORT BLANKET

When I was in high school, I kept a diary for a short time, a few months at most. At the time, I believe I had just come from a summer youth camp for a week held by my best friend's church youth group in Castle Rock, Colorado. I remember being galvanized to go home a different kid, less moody, less depressed, more Godly. I thought keeping a diary would help me. If I could write down my thoughts and the things I struggled with, maybe I could finally get victory over them. Maybe I could understand myself a little better. I am quite sure that I eventually got discouraged in the endeavor because I didn't continue the practice on into adulthood. The diary was put away with my other old writings, poetry and short stories, to gather dust and probably never see the light of day again.

But the diary did come back to haunt me. There was a time, probably a year or two into our marriage, when I came home and Felacia excitedly told me that she had found my diary... and that she had read it and really wanted to talk about it with me. In her mind, finding the diary was very exciting because I had been a very enigmatic husband, hard to know and hard to understand. My go-to emotion was anger, and I'm sure my go-to action was lethargy. But she was desperately trying to "get" me. I definitely played hard to get back then. She was very surprised and quite hurt when my response was one of tremendous rage, as if she had told me she cheated on me or bankrupted us somehow. I got so angry at her, asking her repeatedly how she ever thought it was okay for her to read my diary without asking me. I was furious, and I felt betrayed. She of course was totally surprised at my reaction and shocked at my anger. She truly didn't understand why I would be so angry about it. She thought her reading it would have brought us closer together. I believe she underestimated how deeply embarrassed I was that she had read secret things about myself that I myself had not even read since high school. I racked my brain to imagine what sordid things I may have written about that time that I should be ashamed of. I couldn't remember, but I also could imagine. She kept trying to plead her case that it wasn't a bad thing for her to have read the diary because we were married, and there shouldn't be secrets between us; I would not be placated, and I in fact demanded that she give the diary to me. As I remember, I took the diary out to the grill in the backyard, doused it with lighter fluid, and burned it up.

I was acting as if a witch had cast a spell on the writings, and I had to destroy it at all costs. During those days, my secrets were a comfort blanket, and I guarded them fiercely. I kept pornography to myself, preciously, like Gollum with his ring. I kept my fears, of being the head of our house, of not being good enough, or Christ-like enough, to myself. I kept my emotions to myself. I kept ME to myself. And my young, innocent wife was suffering, trying to make a life with a man she never knew and was beginning to feel like she'd never know. I was always very guarded with her. I was generally guarded with everyone. I think she expected that at some point, in some way, I would let my guard down, at least with her. She wasn't trying to get me to let my guard down so she could rush in for the kill. She just wanted to know who I was. Felacia is, as I have said, a very genuine person. I've rarely known her to be deliberately vindictive or intentionally mean. She's just been honest and straightforward. I've never had to wonder what she thinks. She'll tell me. She was unguarded in those days. I was quite an attack dog, wounded and ever on the defense. I think I was very much driven by shame, and well versed in that shame by the time we met. On one of our first dates, we sat down and had drinks at her favorite coffee shop, and she pointedly asked me, "Do you have low self-esteem?" out of the blue. I find her sweet innocence to be a beautiful thing now that I know her because I know she asked it as a helper, a person who sees a need and wants to fill it, like the mantra on the animated movie *Robots*. I thought she was being intrusive at the time, the same way I thought she was being intrusive in reading the diary. I told her the diary was mine and she should have asked me to read it.

I refused to let her explain her point of view and instead chose to see her as controlling and invasive. That diary was a point of contention for many years between us. The feelings behind it were longstanding and deep. I'd become a very embarrassed, closed-off man with lots of secrets. I was constantly angry and defensive, and often accused Felacia of trying to shame me or put me down in some way or another. Anger had become a comfort blanket as well, one that was frayed and unprotective, and one that was increasingly fraught with sharp edges. I felt that her "invasion" of my privacy was unjust, and my deepest desire in that regard was that she admit that she was wrong to have read it. That would have been Justice to me. We must be careful when seeking justice. It is a two-edged sword that can cut on its way back into the sheath. The more ashamed I felt, the more I lashed out. The more I lashed out, the more I felt ashamed. It was a vicious cycle, and I was constantly apologizing. I believe I was always apologizing because I was always seeking an apology. I was always seeking Justice.

Justice seekers must always be careful. The justice we seek from others is the same justice that others may seek from us one day. Justice seeks to be impartial and fair by the law, but often laws are bent by the very people that make them. I viewed it as unjust for her to read my diary, yet to me she was an open book if I was willing to take time to read her. She was totally unguarded, to a fault even, to the point that she'd allow herself to get hurt if it meant people felt close to her. I felt it unjust that she was near her family when mine seemed so far away, when in reality, I often pushed my extended family away just as I pushed hers away. I sought Justice but gave little, and in turn I became unmerciful.

Eventually, I resolved to see the diary incident as a deep and unnecessary wound, a rift I created between us. I can honestly say that as I have been writing this book and allowing Felacia to read it and share her thoughts with me, that I believe God is redeeming some of the great damage I did by my reaction to her reading what I had written back then. I want her to know me now. I want her to see me, good and bad, if it helps her in some way. I want her to understand the man she married so she can know how grateful I am that she stayed, that she hung in there with me despite the man I often showed her that I was. I was holding on to a comfort blanket; she was trying to give me a clean quilt of her own making instead, something we could share together to keep us both warm and happy. I have always said the greatest miracle God ever performed is a changed life, and I pray that if nothing else, the things written here are a testament to a changed man, and the power of God to change men, and the power of those humans who stay, and love, even when it hurts to do so. These pages are my comfort blanket to my wife Felacia, and a new diary of sorts, for her and I to read, and to understand each other.

CHAPTER 12

GOD HATES DIVORCE

In a recent conversation, I learned that 80% of divorces between men and women are initiated by women. I, of course, had to verify that by Googling it. According to the Whitley Law Firm website, nearly 70% of divorces are initiated by women, and among college-educated women, that number jumps to a staggering 90%! The law firm went on to state three main reasons why women tend to be the main ones filing for divorce.

The number one reason is because Women are more likely to feel held back by the marriage. It states that women work outside the home more now than perhaps any other time in history, yet married women still do the bulk of the housework and the childcare for the family. It also states that many men feel psychological distress if their wives made more than 40 % of the total household income. I fully believe this to be the case. I can remember during the 17 years that Felacia worked, when the kids were not yet in school and later when they were in school, I fully expected that Felacia was going to be responsible for finding a babysitter when either one of us had any change in our work schedule, even though we were both working. Somehow, I thought she was "better at that stuff". I also left it to her to do nearly all the cooking for both of us and the kids, and I was at a tremendous loss if I ever had to figure out dinner. I can remember a period when finances always seemed to be an issue, and I felt like we were eating out too much. We ended up having a meeting with our pastors where I complained that she wasn't cooking often enough for us as a family. Keep in mind that this was still many years before she came off the job, so she was expected to cook in the midst of all her many other "wifely" duties. There were many, many times after that day that she expressed hurt that I would throw her under the bus to our pastors that way, portraying her as if she were being neglectful of the family. I know at the time that I was so consistently angry and uptight that her complaints about my actions went in one ear and out the other. I would also agree that the issue of who brought more money in often came up, mainly due to the fact that she started off making more than I did at the beginning of our marriage; it would again be many, many years before I became the higher earner of the two of us. This too became an issue and a point of contention for us, because it didn't take long into our marriage for me to become quite competitive with her. All these issues in concert began to deeply wound our relationship.

The second reason was also a massive contributor to our marital stress and strife: Women often take on more of the emotional burden. This was most definitely the case for us. Felacia took on nearly all of the emotional burden of our marriage alongside the other marital weight she was carrying. I am an introvert and not the best verbal communicator even on my best days: I'm the sort who can comfortably sit in silence for long periods at a time, even if someone else is there with me. This is especially true if there is any animus or conflict present. I believe many men struggle with the vulnerability that is required for true emotional health as I have struggled; it is something that has not been taught effectively to us and is often touted as a "Woman's" trait. As a result, Felacia often had to lean on her family and some good friends for the emotional support she so desperately needed. I on the other hand just retreated further into myself. Felacia would often plead with me to solicit more solid male friendships, asking me to find guys to share the burden of manhood with like she shared the woes of a married woman with her female friends, with those friends who would listen, pray, and understand. I always shook the need for such connections off as unnecessary. I was the Punisher. I work alone. The wounds got deeper because I got more emotionally constipated and angry.

The third reason is because Women no longer tolerate consistent unacceptable behavior. The article states that modern women, who do not often need their husbands in the same way for financial security, are not nearly as willing to put up with the Jekyll and Hyde change in their husbands after marriage. The man of romance on whom the sun never sets becomes the werewolf in the dim light of the moon's glow, but the modern wife is more Buffy the Vampire Slayer than June Cleaver, and often the marriage ends. That's exactly where things were headed for us. I had been told by Felacia for years that I needed to seek counsel about my anger and bitterness and find a resolve with my pornography struggles. I always chose to ignore the problem and the need for any help. Finally near the middle of 2022, when our daughter was graduating high school, the specter of divorce was beginning to make more sense. Our nest was soon to be empty. What would be the purpose of continuing the charade any longer? Both our children would soon be gone into their own adult lives, and what would Felacia and I really have left together? Again, for what seemed to me the millionth time, she spoke of her desire for divorce. And again, I really was considering it. But this time, I was genuinely, truly thinking about the possibility and the need for a divorce. I also began to feel that I could no longer tolerate consistent unacceptable behavior. At this point, I had been the primary breadwinner for several years. I had been what I considered faithful and had made every effort to give Felacia and our children a comfortable life. I had begun to feel that she was deeply ungrateful for all my efforts to be a "good" man. I was getting weary in well-doing.

When she presented the idea this time, I told her I was going to seek a lawyer the next Monday. And I said she'd have to get a job because I was no longer willing to support her in the same way as I had been supporting her the past few years, being the sole income. For perhaps the first time in our history, I was truly not being vindictive in what I said. I was being honest. She had a meltdown that day and I ended up coming home early from work at her request. We began the first of many talks and rows and arguments about where we stood with each other; we finally decided that, for the sake of our soon-to-graduate daughter, we would revisit the need to divorce by the following August, after we had sent her away to college. It only made sense, and deep down, I think we were both relieved to put that possibility away for a while longer. Something in my heart was changing however, something that had never changed in any of the other myriad of times before when divorce had been discussed between us. Something had changed in me. I began to see what Felacia had always talked about. I had never quite put in the emotional 110% she needed from me, and she needed me to, now more than ever. Like most men, I regarded the fact that I provided financially in greater and greater measure as the years of our marriage progressed as a sign that I was doing better by us. She told me before that money meant very little in the scheme of things. She would often say that she didn't need my money; she could make her own. I believe what I couldn't hear was what lay behind what she was saying: she didn't need my money, but she did need my heart. She wanted me. She didn't need me. But she wanted me, an emotionally healthy me.

It eventually became clear to me that what she had always asked me to do was very simple, yet I had always cast the need away as unnecessary. She wanted me to find a way to connect myself with my emotions. Deal with the hurts. Accept and connect with the anger. I had always made vague promises to go get therapy, but this time, I took the time to get a therapist, and we talked about a lot of the things I'd always kept tucked away, even from Felacia, the one closest to me. I had a college-ruled notebook I would take to my sessions, and I quickly filled it with notes about myself and Felacia regarding our emotional needs and challenges. My therapist had me to read a book that opened my mind in a million ways to who I was emotionally and why I had become that way. The book was *How We Love* by Milan and Kay Yerkovich. I highly recommend this book to everyone, even if they're not married. It was truly a revelation. I quickly realized how badly I needed to get these things, these feelings out. It had been far too long... indeed, I nearly lost my marriage because of it.

Therapy opened a door; I walked through it. Felacia and I began to talk through our issues together, and more importantly, I began to slowly turn a corner, and I'm still on that journey even now. I truly believe I did what I could do, and God met me in the middle. I cannot say what definitive change occurred or when. I just know that I began to feel less angry over the next year. Things that had always infuriated me seemed a little less infuriating as we talked about them. Both Felacia and I resolved to change our approach to each other in various ways. I vowed to be more honest, more forthright. She worked at responding more gently. Instead of seeing her as always having it all together, I began to see how truly fragile she was and had always been. It became more imperative for me to protect her and her open book of feelings, which were always at the mercy of others. I was learning to be kind and not just nice.

I believe my ultimate resolve at the time of our impending divorce was this: I was not willing to part ways with my beloved wife Felacia unless I felt I had gone to every length to be the best man I could be. I knew in my heart of hearts that I had not truly exhausted every effort to be the best man I could be for her and for me. Maybe all of us as men, as we marry, should worry less about who is going to be our best man at the wedding; we should instead seek to be the best men we can be for our wives, and for ourselves. I made a deal with myself. I would do my utmost, I would do absolutely everything as a man and as a husband to be the man Felacia envisioned me to be when she said "yes" to me. If I knew that at my core I had become the very best man and husband I could be for her and she still was disgruntled or angry or seemed unhappy, I would then feel free to leave her in good conscience, having done all I could conceivably do to be a good Joel to her. I would not feel that I abandoned her without trying to be my best self for both of us. I could part ways with her honorably. I knew at that time that I had not done my very best. That, to me, was not in question. I knew I could try, however. Knowing my marital fate was in my hands was a comfort to me because I believed that God truly is the changer of hearts. God does hate divorce, but He also hates misery. I knew if I asked God to change my stony, hard heart, He would. If there is one thing I know, it is the fact that married or not, I was miserable in myself and would remain so if something didn't change. The realization was that I wasn't changing for Felacia. I wasn't even changing for God Himself. I was changing for me, but both Felacia and the Good Lord would reap the benefits of that change alongside me.

The lovely thing about those changes and victories is that they can be small yet so rich. It was during those tentative months when our marriage was hanging by just the thinnest of threads that Felacia expressed to me one day how much she disliked having to do so much laundry, and how she would be relieved that our daughter, who was headed off to college in a few days, would be responsible for her own clothes from then on. It was as if the very angels in Heaven allowed me to see the slightest wisp of unburdening in my sweet wife's face and I immediately said, "Well, I'll start washing and drying my own clothes too." Felacia looked at me as if I'd just given her a diamond necklace. I felt a strange pleasure in her response, in my ability to lighten her load in this way. "Are you sure?", she asked. I was sure. It only made sense. We were becoming a house full of adults, with the emotional intelligence of adults. Adults can do their own dirty laundry. I now realize we had been airing out our dirty laundry to each other for quite a while now, had even begun to wash a lot of that dirty laundry together, and the air between us was beginning to smell sweet again.

CHAPTER 13

NEEDS IMPROVEMENT

There is one anger trigger that I would venture to say every human being struggles with, whether he is a daytrader on Wall Street, or she is a computer programmer in Silicon Valley. He might be a tribesman in the Australian bush, or she's a runway model in Paris. No matter our station in life, income or lack thereof, number of likes and follows, or number of years following our likes, we all run headlong into that great brick wall of disappointment that has two grand words spray-painted on it: "NEEDS IMPROVEMENT!" Many of us begin life with the most fruitful series of compliments as we take our first steps, hold our bottles of milk with our own tiny hands, and eat a spoonful of solid food for the first time. Even filling a diaper is impressive and celebrated by some parents on their child's first go-'round. The celebration of the mundane when you're a small child can be one of Satan's cruel tricks as you get a little older. We start those early years of school, and slowly the one hundred eighty-degree turn begins as we get that first not-so-stellar grade or the teacher takes our special glittery star off the wall for talking out of turn too much in kindergarten. Some of us may get a letter or note sent home to our parents, notifying them of our unruly behavior in class. Slowly but surely, the carousel of life begins to speed up, but your faithful horse can't match its velocity. You need improvement.

The ultimate assault on our young notion of our value is Santa Claus. A rosy cheeked fat man in red is keeping a tally of whether you've been bad or good all year, and depending on where you fall, you may or may not get what you want for Christmas. And the final nail in the coffin for any genuine good or honesty in the world is when a child realizes that there is no Santa Claus, and that the old man is just a construct some adults use to keep children in line. With some facetiousness, I would posit that the Great Lie causes that disillusionment that many eventually face: why try to improve? Why try to be good for someone that doesn't actually exist to care about you either way?

I've heard the idea expressed about playing a game where you repeatedly get close to the goal, but then some phantom entity moves the goalpost. You feel like you're succeeding, but suddenly realize you need improvement. The game is rigged. I remember playing football in the park as kids, on a sunny day, no pads and no real rules. There was always the kid whose dad watched football every Sunday and knew all the rules of the game front to back. That kid would take over what had been a loosey-goosey gathering of children playing some hybrid version of the National Football League by expressing a litany of proclamations on what we were all doing wrong. Many times, as a child would, the football expert seemed to change the rules at will, to suit himself. Often, would-be experts seem to have great confidence in knowing what is required for others to improve; the anger for us all is when we find ourselves outside the narrow circle of what constitutes doing it right. Being good. Succeeding.

Being right can seem like a losing proposition and one that is very hard to achieve. This feeling of not being good enough, of needing improvement, usually left me angry and confused at various stages of my life. If anyone can change the position of the goalpost whenever they decide to, what use is there to playing the game at all? I believe this hopeless attempt to kick a field goal at a goalpost that won't stay still is what leads some to suicide. They lose hope in a rational, fair and just world. There is something in a sane mind, a mind still capable of rational thought, that wants to feel as if it can keep up with the changes and waves of the world. In some sense, we all need to find and adapt our mental and emotional "sea-legs", the ability that seafarers develop to maintain their footing despite the dips and yaws and ups and downs of the ship. We need to feel balanced as human beings, as if even in our weaknesses, we are yet improving.

But the Devil is in the details. There is always a notion that Santa, and everyone else in the wide world, is watching us, waiting for us to fail. The fat man in red with the big bag of presents on his shoulder becomes the skinny creature in red with the horns on his head and the pitchfork in his grip, ready to poke us with shame and derision every time we screw up. It can be a zero-sum game. I remember it being a relief and a revelation when Mom and Dad revealed to us that Santa Claus wasn't real. We were relatively young, and I think in a Christian home at the time, it began to be perceived as dishonorable to God and the sacrifice of His Son to glorify Santa Claus on Jesus' birthday. I recall not being in the least bit disappointed that there was not a Santa Claus because I was conveying my gift wishes to Mom and Dad anyway, plus the fact that we didn't have a chimney no longer mattered if there was no St. Nick. It relieved my young logic to know the truth. Somehow, it was a relief that we weren't shackled to the ever-present eyes of Santa or Satan; neither one had any sway over who we chose to be over that year, and the belief in Christ being born into this world as our Savior had much more meaning to my young mind then, because Christ Himself became the cornerstone of the notion that mankind can improve. He came down to Earth to give man the ability to be better. Jesus Christ gave me sea-legs. He gave me superpowers in a sense. The idea of being greater than a skin color or body type or any other restriction began to grow in unison with having a Savior who cared about me, who saw me as greater than the sum of my parts. He didn't see me or anyone else as needing improvement because He came to Earth to be the improvement for us. The final nail in the coffin was removed, since it had nothing to do with Santa Claus not being real.

Our Goodness is not real. Goodness was the elusive Santa we children were all chasing, as if we were waiting to board the Polar Express. Goodness was a phantom in a sleigh in a place we couldn't visit. Goodness is ultimately God Himself.

We cannot be good. I'm still tempted at times with pornography. Honestly, I have to be very careful what I watch entertainment-wise and also what I see on the internet, like an alcoholic has to be careful around bars and mixed drinks and mouthwash. Pornography is to the eyes and ears what alcohol is to the mouth and liver. I'm still often tempted to blow a fuse, get furiously angry at slights great, small or non-existent. Unchecked anger is to the soul what pornography is to the eyes. I still crave a mixing bowl full of Frosted Mini Wheats and Frosted Flakes combined in equal measure, the Holy Grail of cereal to me especially after 10 PM. I often crave what is not good for me. I'm not good. I'm not nice. But I can be righteous. One of my Sea-Leg verses in the Bible, a verse that ever since I really, truly understood it gave me great hope for my eventual ability to be right with God, was Romans 5:7-8. It reads, "For scarcely will one die for a righteous man, yet perhaps for a good man some would even dare to die. But God commendeth His love toward us in that, while we were yet sinners, Christ died for us." I found it comforting to know that yes, many people in the world would be willing to die for a good man. The problem is that there are very few good men. Even the best of us struggle with jealousy or lust or hate. Being good is the ever-moving goalpost. So what does it mean to be righteous then? Oxford Dictionary defines righteous as "morally right or justifiable; virtuous". Merriam-Webster gives the goalposts the running speed of a gazelle when it defines righteousness as "acting in accord with divine or moral law : free from guilt or sin". So if people might die for a good man, who is inherently good in and of himself, and they probably wouldn't die for a righteous man, who is acting according to moral law, what hope do any of us have?

That is the beauty of verse 8. While we were yet sinners, scrolling through illicit websites, and cussing out the waiter or the neighbor, Christ died for us. He made us righteous. His death made us righteous. Christ said of Himself in Mark 10:18 (21st century KJV)- "And Jesus said unto him, 'Why callest thou Me good? There is none good but One, that is, God'". Jesus was speaking to a rich young man who was inquiring as to how to achieve eternal life, and He made it very clear that even He, Christ Himself, was not good. Only God is good. If the most perfect human that ever lived isn't good enough to be good, there's hope for me. And there's hope for you. The goalpost has stopped moving. The Bible also says that we are clothed in Right-eousness. It's as if it is something we put on, like a robe after a shower. We are cleaned up, and then we are covered up. The need for improvement becomes satisfied outside of ourselves. The search for the elusive "good" man is over, to be replaced with the righteous one. I found great comfort in this because it helped me immensely on my continuing journey out of anger. I don't find myself exhausted in the never-ending effort to improve, to get better, to prove my worth and value to the world. Santa has been skipping my house for the majority of my half a century on this earth, but the great blessing to me is that the other entity in red has no rights in my house either. Those robes of righteousness have covered the need for improvement with a need met.

CHAPTER 14

THE CONFIDENCE OF HUMILITY

Is it possible to be humble and confident at the same time? In the same body and mind?

There was a time when I would definitively answered "No" to that question. It is not possible to be humble and confident in the same body. People are either arrogant or humble, either meek or confident. One cannot be both. I believed that people who came across as confident were generally prideful. They bragged too much. A humble person would be more self-effacing, more self-deprecating. They wouldn't be focused on themselves all the time. It would be quite a while before I came to realize that my general demeanor, one that came across a bit like Eeyore, one that was always down on myself and my ability to take life by the horns and run with it, was in its own way a very self-centered and arrogant way of seeing myself in relation to the world around me. There is nothing less attractive than a person who constantly sees themselves as "less than". People of confidence often meet the confident energy of other confident people, while the rest of us feel left in the lurch.

I can remember when I first moved to Alabama, I naively believed I would be met by Confederate flags and burning crosses, and I also arrogantly believed that my having earned a college degree naturally made me smarter than most everyone I was likely to meet. All the while, I was quiet-natured and even-tempered to those on the outside looking in, at least until they got to know me. I had a vast trove of prejudices of my own when I graduated college, and millions of pre-conceived notions about how the world works. This is the arrogance of ignorance. It's easy to be an expert on the world and its ways when you've never really engaged the world on a primal level. There was a time for instance when I was racing in my little maroon 1993 Chevy Cavalier down an old country highway in Alabama. This was early in my dating life with Felacia, when I was still living in New Orleans. I was headed to her family home to visit her. There's a certain stretch of Highway 43 that she always warned me not to speed through, because it was known as a speed trap. I was bulletproof at the time, so I had no regard for my speedometer or for being aware of any cops around. I had a pretty good chip on my shoulder coming to Alabama as a re-cent college graduate anyway, and especially toward law enforcement; sometimes I wonder if that chip on my shoulder was a result of my college experience, which is, IMHO, partly an effort to taint the minds of the young into a collective anger. At any rate, I was cruising along, listening to one of my Christian hip hop CDs, when I saw the red and blue flashing lights behind me. The policeman pulled me over and gave the usual spiel about how fast I was going and how I needed to slow down, and then he summarily gave me a ticket. Now, he never dragged me out of the car, he never pulled his gun, and he didn't stand there drawling at me with a piece of wheat at one corner of his mouth. But I was still indignant. When I got to Felacia's parents' house, I of course angrily told her how the unjust cop pulled me over for speeding because I was Black. She replied, "No, he pulled you over because you were speeding."

Sometimes, in our cloud of arrogance, our natural ability to reason becomes cloudy and what should be obvious to us becomes mentally opaque and unclear. I was in fact speeding, but I had developed 24 years of experience at being confident in my oppression. I was always ready to be angry at someone or something; my anger just wasn't an outward one because that was not the image that I wanted to project. My anger was a seething undercurrent. It was the Hulk's secret to how he was always able to become the Hulk: he was always angry. I moved to Alabama with that oppressed confidence, the overconfidence of the underdog. I had told myself for so long the narrative that I was being held back by some outward force, that I didn't see how arrogant I really was. I didn't see the person other people were seeing in me. It was overconfidence that led me to quit my job in the space of two days to move to Alabama for a job at a shipyard. I had worked in a law library at my former university and had never done any manual labor to that degree. I was entering a welding school. I got the job at the shipyard, but, after having moved into Felacia's aunt's home, I quit that job after three months, and it was another two months after that before I got another job. What a lazy, inconsiderate bum I was then!

It was that same overconfidence when I was eventually blessed to get a good job at a power plant in our area that led me to assume that I would, with my all-powerful English degree, be able to ace any test they gave me on the job. As it turned out, I embarrassingly flunked the test to become an assistant mechanic twice before I finally passed. I was devastated and my confidence sorely shaken after those two failures. Mechanical work did not and does not come naturally to me, even though I have done it now for 23 years. I've learned in those years to become a decent mechanic. That's what true humility should do; it should allow us to gain skill in necessary areas of our lives while also gaining good character in our minds. Our bodies and our minds grow in tandem. Feeling inadequate isn't always a bad thing. It can often challenge us to want to be better. At the time I was taking those tests, I was beginning to feel like I wasn't going to make it as a mechanic. I felt very inadequate. How was I going to feed my family? Looking back on it now, I wouldn't trade anything for those experiences, and I wouldn't change anything about them. I needed to develop the humility I was sorely lacking. That is the funny thing about ignorance: it can give you a false sense of confidence in things you know little to nothing about. I was beginning to see clearly how much I did not know... and how much I needed to learn. It's been with age and a bit of wisdom that I am coming to terms with what I don't know.

That coming to terms can create something beautiful in us: the desire to learn. When we begin to humble ourselves, we become aware of the vast realm of things that are there for us to see and experience. I had vowed after quitting the shipyard that I hated welding and burning and would never do either again. However, as a mechanic at the power plant, one of our on-the-job classes was a welding class. We were privileged to have an excellent welding teacher, who taught us how to see the bead of our welds as we were welding, and I realized how much it reminded me of how much I loved drawing when I was a kid. That welding class remains one of my favorite On-the-job classes I've ever taken. And all from a trade that I had decided I hated. The humility of accepting what you don't know gives you the confidence that you can learn what you don't know. My father-in-law is an excellent mechanic, and something he often said was that if a man made it, he could learn to fix it. Felacia said he would take things apart as a kid so he could figure out how to rebuild them. He has always inspired me to be able to fix things and build things. I've become halfway decent at that over the years. My mom has inspired my writing. She writes beautifully, and she often wrote poetry that she would share with us when we were young. She also read to us a lot as kids, so I've always loved to read. My Dad shared his love of music and movies and the arts with all of his three kids. My sister got a degree in music from Loyola in New Orleans, and my brother, who also got his English degree from Loyola, was becoming well-known as a hip-hop artist in Colorado at the time of his death. He'd even traveled to Singapore to perform. Long live Bionik Brown! I have since passed my love of music and movies on to my own kids, just as Felacia has passed her singing gift to our daughter. These are all skills and hobbies we learned. The willingness and ability to learn is a true sign of humility in any person. People who know everything don't need to learn anything, and people who won't learn anything don't know anything.

The confident person is the one who is comfortable with what they don't know, and so they become comfortable with what they can learn. These are the people that enter a room with hands extended, ready to meet and greet the people they don't know and haven't met. Every interaction becomes an opportunity. A meeting can become a match. Humility is not marked by a lack of talent or skill or beauty or ability. You can have all those things and still be humble. Humility is marked by the skill of knowing that there is always more, more to learn, more to see, more to do, more to experience. The more I have reached out to learn, the more humbled I've become by what I don't know. But the joy of learning replaces the embarrassment of the proud.

I don't have to know everything to be viable in this world. I still have no reputation to uphold.

CHAPTER 15

SUNSET, OR A FINAL RESOLVE

The last time I got angry at my Dad was after the last time I ever saw him alive.

It was September 2005. Dad and Mom had been living in our town for about three months. They'd moved nearby to be closer to us since our son was only four years old and our daughter was a baby still, almost nine months old. Dad was a doting grandfather back then, and he was eager to be around his grandkids, and so he'd made what would be his final abrupt move from one state to another with Mom in tow. I don't think at the time that I realized how excited he was to be a grandpa, because I'd gotten so used to what I believed were his whims and restlessness. He seemed to feel that he and Mom really needed to make the move to be near us; I think he knew he didn't have very long to live.

Mom and Dad rented a small house in Chickasaw, a little town near us, maybe a ten-minute drive, and we would see them regularly with the kids. Dad started a job at a local car rental, and Mom found employment at a mental facility nearby as an LPN. They settled in quickly and pretty well it seemed, even purchasing an old Toyota Camry and a 12-year-old Jeep Cherokee so they could get to their respective jobs. I was working at the power plant by then, and Felacia and I were in the groove of raising our small children, youth pastoring at our church, and trying our best to keep our heads above water as a married couple with very little time for each other. It was nice having Mom and Dad close by again, but deep down, I was feeling the stress, the pressure of worrying whether they were going to be okay. Somehow, I still fought with the idea that I should be responsible for my parents, or maybe more that they should be responsible for me. I think mentally I was still struggling with the attachment of a man/child to my parents while trying to still wrap my head around the idea of being married to Felacia and responsible for her and our kids. The same strange pressure I felt on our wedding night about driving in the Cadillac was the same strangely foreign pressure I was feeling with Mom and Dad living nearby again. This was in no way a pressure they were putting on me; I was creating the pressure myself.

I remember the night before Dad died, Felacia and I took the kids over to visit with them. I'm sure Mom made a nice dinner for us all, and Dad and I sat in a small room where the television was. He was watching a Tyler Perry play, and he laughed with his whole body, as he always did. He still loved to laugh, even though he was getting to a stage where he seemed to sleep a lot, and his belly had grown quite round, and very hard. He was well into the final stages of congestive heart failure, but neither I nor Felacia knew, and he never talked about it. Maybe it was because I still really saw myself as his kid in a way that I was oblivious to the obvious signs that he wasn't feeling well and hadn't been for quite a while. I just sat there enjoying his hearty laughter with the fascination of a kid, a kid who had to get up for work early that morning.

The next morning, I was headed up Highway 43 to work, usually a quiet drive from town with little traffic, when I noticed a Toyota Camry on the middle ground between the north and southbound sides of the highway; the Camry was a silver color that was almost a shade of gold, and it had the same temporary dealer plates that Mom and Dad's newly purchased Camry had. I was almost positive that it was their car. Even though it had been recently purchased from a very shady small used car dealer in town, they almost immediately began having trouble with it. Seeing it abandoned as a broken-down car would be wasn't a surprise. I just knew it was their car, and Mom's new job was along the same route that I drove to work. She would have been driving that car. The Jeep they had was in better shape, so I wondered why Dad didn't send her to work in the better car. I was prematurely getting angry at what I felt was his irresponsibility and neglect of Mom to send her in the faulty Camry, so I resolved to call him and ask about it when I got home from work that evening.

2005 was during the days pre-iPhone, when a cellphone was not permanently attached to every person's hand or wrist in the free world, so I had to wait until I got home to call Dad. I had a 40-minute drive home from work, and as I drove and stewed, I got more and more angry. Nothing had really changed, I thought. As I became more cognizant of what it meant to have a family, to be beholden to and responsible for the life and safety of not only your wife, but your children, I somehow became an expert on what Dad should have been doing as a husband at that stage of his life. I was still ignorant. You should have gotten a better car or cars since you had to go to work,

I thought, but of course, I had no idea as to whether they had the finances to do so. "You should have either let Mom take the good vehicle or driven her to work", I chided Dad in my mind, not at all thinking that there may have been a reason he didn't drive her that day. At any rate, I called Dad when I got home. He sounded very winded on the phone; I think his poor system was just filling up with water as often happens with congestive heart failure, and it was getting harder for him to breathe. I asked him if that was their Camry I saw on the roadside, and in fact, it was. I don't recall what the particular issue was, but Dad told me was going to talk to the dealer who sold it to him the next day. I didn't say much about it all to Dad, didn't chastise him at all, but I know I was very angry about the whole situation when I got off the phone. I'm sure Felacia got an earful from me that night.

We went to bed. I had to be up early to head back to work. I sleep very deeply and so I didn't hear the phone ring those several times during the night. At some point, Felacia woke me up with a lot of concern in her voice and worry on her face. She said Mom had left a message on our answering machine, quite a few messages in fact, saying that Dad wasn't doing well, that he'd collapsed on the floor, foaming at the mouth.... that the ambulance came, and that it took forever for the ambulance to arrive because of the weird location of the house they were living in. Dad was at the hospital, and we needed to come right away. When we arrived, Dad was already gone. The nurses quietly led us to the bare room where he was lying on a gurney with a sheet over his body up to the shoulders. He was laying on his back, almost as if he was asleep. His shoulders were bare, and hairy like they'd always been. He had my big head, or I have his, and he still had his salt and pepper hair and that ever-present black, thick walrus mustache. That was my Dad laying there, it was undeniable. I went to bed that night and he was still with us. I woke up early in the wee hours of the morning, and he's gone. Just like that.

I began to realize that the end of my time with him was tainted by anger. I couldn't take it back. I had planned to call him that next day and tell him how angry I was that he let Mom get stranded the way he did, though I later found out that he didn't leave her stranded to begin with. In my misguided anger, I had been feeling like he was being irresponsible with his decision-making since they'd moved to town, and I'd grown increasingly frustrated with Dad, deep down, as always. Somehow, I know, had I been honest and forthright with him, he would have been receptive to my feelings. The sometimes moody and stubborn man that I always loved as my special, unique, larger-than-life Dad was changing, becoming softer in ways that even I could tell. I know now that he was most likely feeling a pressure far greater than any pressure I was feeling at the time; he was feeling the shadow of the end, I believe, slowly and quietly creeping up on him like a tiger. The desperation to move to be near us, the seemly rash decision-making, the urgency to spend more time... I think they all stemmed from him knowing that soon he might die, and there wasn't a lot of time to catch up.

As much as I hate to admit it, one of the last times I saw my brother Nathan was just before he and his wife were leaving our house to move to Denver, Colorado after living with us for a month and a half, and I was angry that time too, this time at my brother. He and his wife had to leave New Orleans like many others did in 2005 after Hurricane Katrina, and we were only two hours away, so they left New Orleans to stay with us until the storm blew over. Like everyone who left New Orleans just before Katrina, they fully expected to weather the storm for a few days, then head back home. But it didn't happen that way. Nate and his wife were displaced like many others during that terrible ordeal. I once again felt pressure as Felacia and I took on the responsibility of my younger brother and his young wife for a time. By the end, I'd ended up shouting at him during a long rant in our small kitchen in front of Felacia, our kids, and Nate's wife, telling him how irresponsible and lazy he was, and how he wasn't trying hard enough to take care of his wife and get a new life started for them both.

Nate and I didn't talk for several years after that until he got settled in Denver and invited us to come stay with them after a conference we were attending in Colorado Springs. He wined and dined us, putting us up in a beautiful guest apartment in their very nice apartment building in the Stapleton area of Denver. I think he really wanted us to see how well he was doing, how he was taking care of his wife. How he had made good. Nate wanted me to be proud of him. I really was proud of him, but I don't think I had the sense to tell him before he died. Ironically, I was confronting him about not taking care of his wife the same way I was planning to confront Dad about not taking care of Mom. But I myself was a poor caretaker of Felacia. The very anger that I felt towards what I believed was Dad and Nate's lack of care and concern for the women God placed in their hands was the same anger that was stopping me from taking true care and concern for my own wife.

Time itself has led to my final resolve regarding anger. We don't have much time. The people we care about may not be with us forever, and the people that we shouldn't care so much about may not matter to us at the end of all things. I can waste my energy and strength being angry at politics and world events and news cycles and the latest video of the latest atrocity, or I can spend that same time sorting through whatever feelings are hindering me from living the fullest life I can live. I don't want my final legacy with any person I care about to be a legacy of anger. Time is truly like money, except in one area: while you can make as much money as your hard work and brain will allow, God only gives us a certain allotment of time. We all have the same bank account allotted to us in our time on this earth; we just don't know when that account is going to close for good. The truest and greatest tragedy is to miss the beauty in front of you for the anger behind you. There are so many injustices, so many crimes against God and man that we cannot change, but one of the biggest crimes is to stay angry. It is okay to be angry, but it is not good to stay angry.

Felacia told me of a syndrome called Sundown Syndrome, often experienced by the elderly, mostly those with dementia or Alzheimer's disease, wherein they are triggered by fading light. Sundowning happens in the early evening or into the night, and usually improves by morning. When people are sundowning, they can be agitated, restless, irritable, and disoriented. They may yell or pace around. They may hear and see things that aren't there. They can have wild mood swings. They also become fearful of darkness and shadows and can have trouble separating dreams from reality. Oh, how much these symptoms remind me of how we humans can be when we are angry! So irrational and fearful, often mean and sometimes dangerous. Ephesians 4:26 in the Bible says, "Be ye angry, and sin not: let not the sun go down upon your wrath *(or anger)*". *(*my italics) Felacia and I were talking about how this verse was taught to us as children. It always came across that one should never go to bed angry, but she added more nuance to it. She believes the verse meant that we also should not let our lives end with anger in our hearts toward anyone. I know personally that I've had many a night when I went to bed angry, and often I woke up the same way. There is something about sundown, the end of a day, or the end of a life, that has a great finality to it. This is often a scary and unknown realm that leaves us agitated, and restless, and irritable, and emotionally disoriented. We don't know what is to come. The future is unknown, and it is a future in a realm that is unfamiliar to us.

The comforting aspect of Ephesians 4:26 is that it does not chastise us for being angry. It just tells us to sin not. I believe the sin is in holding that anger over to another day, a fresh day. Anger is like manna to the Israelites; it's only meant to last for one day before it goes bad. The lovely thing about anger is that it truly is a kinetic emotion; I can wake up and the anger has turned into a resolve for some sort of positive change. I can let my mind, my dreams, and the Spirit of God himself transform that anger from the secondary emotion that it should be to whatever the primary feeling was that I was having that led to that anger, so I can deal with it. The sun doesn't have to go down on my wrath. Lamentations 3:22-23 tells us that, " It is of the Lord's mercies that we are not consumed, because his compassions fail not. They are new every morning: great is thy faithfulness." God's mercy is new every morning. He allows the sun to go down. He allowed the event or the person or the happening that made us angry. But He allows the sun to rise again on a new day, with new victories, new challenges, new mercies... maybe, if we can and will let Him, we can allow the happening to become a healing, a bettering of who we are and what we experience.

Every sundown is followed by a sunrise. I don't want it to be said of me that I died angry or let someone die while I was angry with them. I have had a lot of sundowns in my life, but I'm not going to continue to have Sundown Syndrome in my emotional life because of it. God's son has risen, and the sun still rises too. If I happen to face my final sunrise with Felacia's hand in mine, surrounded by my son and my daughter and their families, even the setting sun will be a sweet one.

CONCLUSION

THE ANSWER TO ANGER, OR WHERE I CHOOSE TO DWELL

I have always been a man I do not understand. I don't get ME a lot of the time. Why do I act the way I do in times of stress? Why do I retreat from conflict? Why do I get so angry when I have a conflict with someone else? In examining and attempting to understand myself, I have often thought of myself as emerging out of a cave emotionally and relationally, my dark-adjusted eyes squinting and watering in the light. I imagine myself as an isolated, lonely creature who has managed to find a dry, warm place of solitude in a cold, hard world. I have a place to hide myself from other people, like Quasimodo hid in Notre Dame. My own little cave. It is the enneagram 9 version of peace, a peace that is very easy to understand because it involves staying away from everyone, if not physically, then emotionally. It involves never truly being vulnerable. I don't have to understand myself if I'm by myself. There is no one around who needs me to explain "me" to them.

That isolation is a version of peace. Yet this sort of peace never lasts and never satisfies. I have often envied the warmth of people who choose to live the harrowing life of those who decide to connect with others, even at the risk of getting hurt. Those of us who hide in caves envy those who don't. That is the sort of peace that isn't easy for me to understand, a peace that surpasses all understanding as Philippians 4:7 states, a peace that is not easily found in caves and hideaways where one is alone. This is a peace that satisfies. This sort of peace is hard to find for some of us as humans, and I truly believe that is because that sort of peace can only be found one way: through God Himself, in the person of Jesus Christ.

I would venture to say that the peace that surpasses all understanding is made possible by the fact that Jesus allows us to have a peace that doesn't always have to understand or be understood. People that are fearful are often people that don't understand. They don't understand what is happening to them. They don't understand why it happened. They don't understand how to stop it from possibly happening again. They don't understand other people. All these unknown variables often lead to fear. The fear often leads to anger. And the anger leads to loneliness and isolation. We become the misunderstood. We feel like others don't understand us and don't want to understand us. This is the same place Jesus found Himself when He said of His tormentors "Father, forgive them for they know not what they do." Jesus was headed to the cross as a man who was greatly misunderstood. But He created a place in Himself where He didn't have to understand. Jesus was doing the work of Proverbs 3:5- "Trust in the Lord with all thine heart; and lean not unto thine own understanding. In all thy ways acknowledge him, and he shall direct thy paths".

Jesus was choosing to dwell mentally and spiritually in a place where he didn't have to "get" His tormentors or their reasons. And they didn't have to understand Him for Him to be okay. He was living in a place where His mind and spirit were choosing not to be angry. Even in the writing of this book, I have begun to find myself in a place where I am choosing not to be angry. I am choosing to dwell somewhere else, somewhere different, somewhere... better. My life, like the lives of almost all of us, has been marked by the milestones of times and seasons I didn't understand. I didn't get why I couldn't go to the party with Mom and Dad when I was five. I didn't get why Felacia didn't want to ride in the back of that Cadillac with her in-laws instead of happily riding with her brand-new husband on their first few hours as a married couple. I didn't understand why Dad died at 52, or why Nate died at 32. I didn't understand why deep down, I was always angry. I was always angry because I was always afraid. The Bible, in 1 John 4:18 (ESV), says that "There is no fear in love, but perfect love casts out fear. For fear has to do with punishment, and whoever fears has not been perfected in love." God's love for us is perfect, which is hard to fathom in a world of adultery and abuse, a world where we love pizza, and fishing, and Louis Vuitton purses, and our families all with the same abstract version of love that blankets the world like soot after a fire. Perfect love is simple and unexplainable because it needs no explanation. I didn't need to understand my Dad or my brother to love them. I just needed to love them. Later on, I would understand them, as I have grown to understand them after death. I often thought I needed to understand Felacia to love her better, and for her to understand me. I am finding that the more I can learn to just love her, she becomes easier to understand. King Arthur stated it the right way in the film *Camelot*: The way to handle a woman... is to love her. I'm accepting her as she is.

Acceptance is what all of my friends and family need from me. My son needs me to accept the man he is becoming without me trying to steer him to be the man I think he should be, out of fear that he might become the man I was at his age. My daughter needs me to accept her without prejudice, to allow her to develop into the young woman she needs to be. My mom, my sister, my parents-in-law and siblings-in-law, my second father, my friends... they all need me to accept them as they are. We all need to be accepted in the beloved as the Bible says. The more I have been able to accept life and people as they are, the easier it has been to not be angry. I don't need to understand everything to be ok with it. I believe the older I've gotten, the more I realize how much I don't know. And the more I'm good with what I don't know. I'm less afraid of the unknown, and I'm not angry at things I don't know. I have always disliked the unexpected because not knowing made me feel unsure. I developed a habit of trying to be responsible for as little as possible so I wouldn't have to know in case everything fell apart. If I didn't know, I couldn't be blamed, could I?

There is a comfort in the fact that God is All-Knowing, He knows everything to my nothing, and He's not afraid to take the brunt of it all as a consequence of being the One Who Knows. Knowledge doesn't scare God because He understands. I don't have to know everything because I can ask God to reveal the things that I need to know, through prayer. I am a person who has always kept the pool of information that I needed vague and shallow. I never wanted to know so much that I got overwhelmed; I found that to be a confusing place. But not knowing was a place that also felt uncontrolled, a place where I felt I was at the mercy of whatever came along. Now I find that as I know things, I'm also learning to understand them. To do that requires getting close to what I don't know. Getting close to what I don't know requires me to get vulnerable. Yes, I might get hurt. That's what I was afraid of, so I stayed away. When I did get hurt, I got angry. God, however, is a shield for the hurting soul. The closer I get to God, I get less angry.

All of the resolves, all of the changes, all of the growth funnels down to the one thing that even the wisest ruler of all time once said, "Let us hear the conclusion of the whole matter: Fear God, and keep his commandments: for this is the whole duty of man" (Ecclesiastes 12:13-KJV). We are not sinners in the hands of an angry God. We are angry people in the hands of a gracious, loving God, who sent the true and lasting cure for anger in the form of Jesus Christ, a man who got angry, and a man who learned how to deal with His anger. I can be angry. I can also sin not.

God, then, is the true answer to our human struggles with anger.

www.ingramcontent.com/pod-product-compliance
Lightning Source LLC
Chambersburg PA
CBHW051218160726
47994CB00002B/651